River by Design

Essays on the Boise River, 1915-2015

INVESTIGATE BOISE COMMUNITY RESEARCH SERIES
BOISE STATE UNIVERSITY
2015

VOL. 6

The Investigate Boise Community Research Series publishes fact-based essays of popular scholarship concerning the problems and values that shape metropolitan growth.

VOL. 1:
Making Livable Places: Transportation, Preservation, and the Limits of Growth
(2010)

VOL. 2:
Growing Closer: Density and Sprawl in the Boise Valley
(2011)

VOL. 3:
Down and Out in Ada County: Coping with the Great Recession, 2008-2012
(2012)

VOL. 4:
Local, Simple, Fresh: Sustainable Food in the Boise Valley
(2013)

VOL. 5:
Becoming Basque: Ethnic Heritage on Boise's Grove Street
(2014)

VOL. 6:
River by Design: Essays on the Boise River, 1915-2015
(2015)

Todd Shallat and Colleen Brennan, *editors*

Mike Medberry, *associate editor*

Toni Rome, *graphic designer*

Heidi Coon and Nick Canfield, *research associates*

BOISE STATE UNIVERSITY
Center for Idaho History and Politics
1910 University Drive – MS 1925
Boise, ID 83725-1925
tshalla@boisestate.edu
(208) 761-0485
sps.boisestate.edu/publications

About the cover: Arrowrock on the Boise River, completed in 1915, shattered construction records as the nation's first concrete arch gravity dam. In 2015, Arrowrock turns 100 years old amid urban-rural disputes over the health of western rivers and the value of waterfront land.

The School of Public Service at Boise State University
The school provides placed-based programs and publications that inform and transform public policymaking.

ISBN: 978-0-9907363-3-2

cc creative commons

2015

Dedication

The Patricia E. Herman Fund honors the memory of Patricia Elizabeth "Pat" Herman (1960-2014), a native of Salmon, Idaho, and a public servant who cherished the rugged outdoors. The fund supports community-oriented publications via the Center for Idaho History and Politics and the Boise State University Foundation.

Contents

- Introduction 6
- **1** Rain on Snow 8
  Climate change steepens the challenge of forecasting floods.
  Roy V. Cuellar
- **2** Raising Arrowrock 16
  Bigger has always been better for the builders of Arrowrock Dam.
  Richard Martinez
- **3** Water, Earth, and Gender 32
  Two great American writers tell parallel stories of conquest.
  Erin Nelson
- **4** Float, Paddle, and Surf 46
  River sports make a tourist attraction.
  Travis Armstrong
- **5** History along the Greenbelt 62
  Relics and storied places connect Boise to frontier past.
  Doug Copsey, with Todd Shallat
- **6** The Waterfront District 74
  Garden City bridges the river via parks and urban renewal.
  Sheila Spangler
- **7** Crowding the Suburban Floodplain 90
  At Eagle Island, developers build castles on sand.
  Emily Berg
- **8** Daylighting Caldwell 99
  Urban renewal transforms an asphalt floodway.
  Dean Gunderson
- **9** Draining Dixie 110
  An urban-rural alliance is changing the way Boise manages waste.
  Michael Gosney
- **10** Wildlife Preservation 122
  Parks and conservation protect the creatures of the Boise River.
  Mike Medberry
- Selected Sources 132

Introduction

The Great Pyramid of the Boise River—the tallest dam on the face of the Earth, staggering and monumental—overshadowed even the feats of the Pharaohs as an icon of human triumph. So said a man named Moses at the 1915 dedication of Arrowrock Dam. Governor Moses Alexander, Bavarian born, tipped his hat to "the strength of the people" and led the faithful in song. "My Country 'tis of thee," sang the Bavarian Jew in tune with Idaho farmers. Before them the arching Goliath shot streams of water through cast iron valves. One million tons of concrete. Two hundred sixty rail car loads of sand and Portland cement. Plugging and pooling the granite canyon for 18 slackwater miles, Arrowrock held enough water for 200,000 settlers on 240,000 acres, enough water, said Moses, to redeem the Garden lost to the Fall.

This book is about those expectations—about the pyramids we Boiseans build on the Nile of our sagebrush Sahara, about cities and suburbs and other unmovable objects in the path of an invincible force.

Our study is also a centennial tribute. Sunday, October 4, 2015, marks 100 years to the day since the epoch of Big Reclamation dawned on Arrowrock Canyon. Plenty in that time has been said about dams as bulwarks of progress; much less about how Idahoans have coped. The time is nigh for a Boise Valley assessment. Why and for whom have we Boiseans crowded the floodplain, and what yet might we do when tested by the climate-change forecast of more extreme droughts and floods?

Historically, through a valley of Starbucks and Simplots, the river the French called Boisée has braided with polemical streams. The most familiar is an epic of muscular masculine prowess. "It was a man's task," said Boise's *Capitol News* of the 5-year plugging of Arrowrock Canyon. Blasted deep and bolted 90 feet below the surface to a bed of batholith granite, the colossus, added the *Idaho Statesman*, was "strong," "firm," and "robust." The Boise Project Division of the U.S. Bureau of Reclamation boasted, in a 1965 pamphlet, a total cumulative yield of $929 million, mostly alfalfa, beets, and apples. Today, with Anderson Ranch and Lucky Peak plus three big dams on the Payette River, the bureau's Boise Project claims $1.2 billion in annual yield from cattle and crops. Add $13 million from hydroelectricity and $30 million

A row of cast-iron valves shoot water through Arrowrock Dam.

U.S. BUREAU OF RECLAMATION

and crops. Add $13 million from hydroelectricity and $30 million from slackwater beaches and boating. Add $170 million for allegedly sparing the valley damage from river erosion and floods.

But always there are mirages in deserts. The 58-page project history on the bureau's Boise website says nothing about mechanical failures, leaks, or government bailouts. No mention is made of hellish farm labor conditions on Heartbreak Row, the project's hard-luck nickname. No mention of the cost to the fish and the Earth. "We set out to tame the rivers," wrote Marc Reisner in *Cadillac Desert* (1986). "We set out to make the future of the American West secure; what we really did was make ourselves rich and our descendants insecure."

For richer or poorer, the lifeblood of the Boise Valley still freights a heavy tonnage of hope and fear and scientific conjecture. Our book of essays adds urban-suburban concerns. Chapters descend like a tour from the snow above Idaho City to Boise, Garden City, Eagle, Deer Flat, Caldwell, and the Dixie Drain near Parma. The hundred-mile journey showcases people at work to redeem some lost connection to flood lands. Each stop on the tour interprets a braid of the aquatic and artificial, each a social-political construct, each a pyramid to which all Boiseans contribute a stone.

Todd Shallat
Boise, Idaho
May 2015

1 | Rain on Snow

Climate change steepens the challenge of forecasting floods.

by Roy V. Cuellar

September snow had already fallen in the Northern Rockies. A U.S. Department of Agriculture (USDA) snow surveyor in a four-wheel-drive truck was climbing toward tangled wires, sensors, hoses, antennae, and gauges amid a stand of lodgepole pine. Each piece of equipment at SNOTEL site no. 550, atop Jackson Peak just north of Idaho City, was strategically placed and interconnected. "This is the place," said Alex Rebentisch of Boise.

SNOTEL (short for *SNO*wpack *TEL*emetry) is a western network of data collection stations spread across 12 states. The USDA's Natural Resources Conservation Service uses the sites to collect data on snow accumulation to forecast snowmelt. Rebentisch and other SNOTEL technicians scramble when snow comes out of season. In late September 2014, during an early snowfall, they raced up slopes to pump antifreeze into bladder-like precipitation gauges and check the condition of glycol-filled pressure-sensing snow pillows. The rush to beat winter was on.

Snow data drive the balancing act that keeps the Boise River contained while storing irrigation water. The U.S. Corps of Engineers, a flood agency, strives to empty enough reservoir space to handle a sudden snowmelt. The U.S. Bureau of Reclamation, an agency for the irrigators, hopes to store enough reservoir water to weather a cycle of drought. Both agencies impound and release snowmelt according to complex models based on the SNOTEL forecast, but the calculus is shifting as Idaho temperatures rise. The same climatic forces that are shrinking Montana's iconic glaciers have warmed Boise River Valley by more than 2° F since the Corps of Engineers built Lucky Peak Dam. Increasingly, in the mid elevations, spring thaw has shifted from April to March. Stream temperatures have risen nearly 1° F since the 1990s. Idaho's cold water bull trout have declined 11% to 20%.

Snow is but one of many factors changing the flood equation. Suburbs pave over absorbent marshes. Levees narrow the floodway. Silt fills reservoirs. Erosion degrades infrastructure. In the Boise Valley, where water is politics, geography and engineering

conspire with climate to transform the flood-irrigation balance. Warm rains and shorter winters make the snowmelt equations more complex than ever before.

A Contrast in Two Idaho Rivers

High in the Sawtooth Range of the Rocky Mountains in central Idaho, the season of two rivers begins with the first snows of autumn. On the east slope of the range the 425-mile-long Salmon River begins, while on the wetter, west slope the 102-mile Boise River rises. Both rivers are tributaries of the greater Columbia Basin, and each contributes to the fabric of Idaho in a completely different way.

The Salmon River's value is in its wildness, which attracts a steady stream of tourist dollars to the state's economy. Over the past century and a half, the United States has built dams,

Lucky Peak Dam, completed in 1955

diverted streams, and created reservoirs to provide water where it was needed by farms and settlements. By virtue of its remoteness and surrounding rugged terrain, the Salmon River escaped this human interference. Not without controversy, the dynamics of this free and wild river were recognized and, in 1980, Congress created the Frank Church–River of No Return Wilderness to protect this scenic area.

In contrast to the Salmon, the Boise is a river diverted through dozens of log runs and headgates. Five historic dams—Diversion (1909), Deer Flat (1911), Arrowrock (1915), Anderson Ranch (1950), and Lucky Peak (1957)—serve a metro population of about 600,000. With water from the Payette River, now technically part of the Boise Project, the network reclaims about 400,000 acres. Annually, in dollars, the project's surface value is easy to measure: $581 million in crops, $600 million in livestock, $13 million in hydropower, $30 million in boating and fishing fees and other recreational income, $170 million saved from the damage of seasonal floods. Measuring the cost of those benefits is more problematic. "A series of disappointments, misrepresentations, and blasted hopes" was how the Bureau of Reclamation described the project in the 1920s. In the short term, the project sustains farming in the Boise Valley. Whether those benefits of dams outweigh the longer-term expense of maintaining the systems is a question hotly debated in Idaho's contested West. Although the added values of these structures are hard to measure, one variable must be measured as accurately as possible—snow.

Measuring Snowpack

To effectively measure snow beyond anecdotal amounts is a scientific process. Because of significant scientific advances over the past 100 years, this process has become more precise, allowing crops to grow where none had before, cities to be built along corridors that once flooded unpredictably, and floodways to be terraformed into parks and urban streets. Some cities, like New Orleans, are famous for their floodplain locations. In the 21st century, Idaho's capital city, Boise, is also a product of modern river engineering.

Taking snow course samples at Mores Creek Summit

Unlike rivers in the eastern half of the continent, the rivers of the American West are dependent on winter snows and a snowpack that lasts into summer. In some areas this snowpack is nil, whereas in the high Cascades snow can accumulate to depths of 30 to 40 feet. In some years, up to 80% of the water that flows in the Boise River began as snow.

The first snow survey courses date back to 1906 when Dr. James Church, a hydrologist with the University of

Nevada, Reno, began to document the relationship between accumulated mountain snowpack and watershed stream flows in the lower elevations. By refining early Russian technology, Church improved the technique by which the amount of water contained in snowpack (referred to by scientists as the *snow water equivalent*) is measured. Soon after Church developed his new technique, the USDA took note and began to develop snow courses of their own across the mountainous West. Today data are collected at more than 1,600 locations in 10 western states. As a result, hydrologists are able to make reliable stream flow predictions that individuals and businesses can plan around.

Not all reaches of the Boise Basin are as remote as the west slope of the Sawtooth Range where the Middle Fork of the Boise River rises. Depending on the snow cover, some locations are easily accessible year round by tracked or wheeled vehicles, offering excellent snowpack data collection points. Some of the sites are manual stations, set out along a course easily accessed by snowmobile and snowshoes, whereas others are electronic.

A USDA snowpack measurement station above Idaho City

Beginning in 1977, the Natural Resources Conservation Service of the USDA began converting many locations to SNOTEL sites. The snowpack at these sites is measured electronically by solar-powered instruments that then transmit data by meteor burst telemetry across long distances to two master stations—one in Boise, Idaho, the other in Dugway, Utah. Depending on the weather event or time of year, data may be transmitted hourly in bits and bytes of binary code by a system designed specifically for computers to exchange data in real-time nanosecond bursts, thus conserving the power of the stations' solar-charged batteries during the darker days of winter.

El Niño and La Niña

"If everything was normal, you wouldn't need me," said Ron Abramovich of the Natural Resources Conservation Service. On October 21, 2014, at a professional conference in Boise, Abramovich sought to explain drier winters and warmer springs. Rain-on-snow events, he continued, occur when unseasonably warm temperatures follow mountain snowstorms. Early spring in the Boise Mountains has become increasingly common.

Shifting winds may also be a factor, according to Abramovich. Wet winds hit the mountains from two directions—from Washington-Oregon and from the California Southwest. Westerly systems bring the snow to Bogus Basin. Southwesterly influxes from California are affected by a 3- to 7-year weather cycle called the El Niño Southern Oscillation. El Niño, the warmer phase of the broader climatic cycle, brings moist air over the Pacific Ocean from the equator. La Niña, the colder phase, brings weather extremes of flooding and drought. La Niña often dumps snow in the Northern Rockies. El Niño hits harder in the Sierra Nevadas and the Upper Midwest.

El Niño's turbulent heat transfer from the winds to the snow surface causes condensation and melting. This process increases the exchange of two kinds of heat: sensible and latent. Both raise the water available for runoff to lower elevations where the ground is thawed. This in turn leads to extensive sediment transport, downstream flooding, and the potential for further mass wasting in the form of land and rock slides. Frozen soil prevents water from being absorbed in the ground and quickens the flow of runoff.

The effects of El Niño and La Niña

In forested and vegetation-covered areas, natural shade helps to keep temperatures cooler and wind speeds lower. In essence, these areas can be broken down into three vegetation subclasses: the higher canopied conifer forest, the aspen stands, and the sage class, which provides the least shading. These covered locations generate less water available for runoff than adjacent open areas experiencing the same rain-on-snow event.

Climate Change and the Danger of Floods

In 1996-1997, at Reynold's Creek in Owyhee County, USDA hydrologist Danny Marks closely followed the dynamics of rain on snow. The warm December storm brought 3.47 inches of precipitation, most of it rain. The daily flow of Reynold Creek increased 50-fold.

A U.S. Geological Survey hydrologic technician measuring streamflow

The year 2011 set Idaho records for rain-on-snow runoff flooding. In March, 26 SNOTEL stations reported record-breaking precipitation. Warm rains melted the snow about 2 weeks earlier than SNOTEL forecast. In April, between 6,000 to 8,000 feet in elevation, temperatures reached 70 °F. The heat in the Boise Valley reached 90 °F. Two inches of rain in the last week of April flood the Boise River Greenbelt. "It was easier to be a water manager or farmer back in the '60s and '70s,"

Abramovich explained. Today in the chaos of unpredictable weather, the old formulas no longer apply.

Monsoon rains, hard to predict, complicate SNOTEL forecasts. A heavy rain in August can be welcome relief near the end of the irrigation season. In 2014, August rains in Boise Basin were heavy enough to rival the moisture of May. For water storage, nevertheless, summer monsoons are inconsequential compared with the importance of snow.

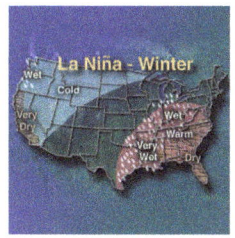

Bracing for La Niña

Conclusion

As the Boise River rolls downhill from the Sawtooth and Boise Mountains, it shows none of the peril that its snowpack holds. It is a charming river to bike or hike along on the warmest, sunniest days of the season. But upstream, as winter wanes, the impact of falling rain on sodden snow presents far more challenging conditions. How will the agencies deal with water retention systems nearing capacity, reservoirs aging and filling with sediment, uncertain climatic conditions, and close to a million people living downstream when a sudden, voluminous, unseasonal deluge threatens to overtop reservoirs? Who can say, but you might want to keep your tennis shoes under your bed.

ROY V. CUELLAR is a retired pilot and the father of three daughters, all graduates of Boise State University. Cuellar graduated from Boise State University with a bachelor's degree in applied science with a minor in history and a concentration in geoscience.

Todd Shallat and Mike Medberry contributed to this chapter.

2 | Raising Arrowrock

Bigger has always been better for the builders of Arrowrock Dam.

by Richard Martinez

Dedicated in 1915, Arrowrock Dam was the "engineering marvel of its time." Headlines in Boise City, Idaho, proudly stated, "Arrowrock, Highest Dam in the World." That record held until 1932, when the height of the Owyhee Dam in eastern Oregon surpassed it. However, pride for the dam continued, as reflected in the poem "Arrowrock Speaks," published in the *Idaho Statesman* in 1932: "Dependent upon me is an empire in the Boise Valley/I was built to store water to irrigate farm lands/Not for Beauty."

Today, the 350-foot dam above the city of Boise remains the centerpiece of the U.S. Bureau of Reclamation's Boise-Payette Project. The Boise part of the project serves five irrigation districts with a total storage capacity of 1,793,600 acre-feet. Its three power plants have a total capacity of 50,200 kilowatts. Its 300,000 acres of irrigated crop- and rangeland yield mostly alfalfa, corn seed, fruit, beets, potatoes, and other row crops. The project also provides flood protection for a fast-growing metropolitan statistical area of 616,000.

In 2008, the U.S. Congress identified Arrowrock Dam, just upstream from Lucky Peak Reservoir, as an "aging federal structure of concern" and in 2015, the U.S. Army Corps of Engineers aims to prepare a draft environmental impact statement to study raising the impoundment by 74 vertical feet. The complexities involved in raising Arrowrock Dam bring together many legal authorities and present some of the hardest questions we face in modern politics—those of economics, safety, and natural resources.

Aging Arrowrock and Ecosystem Restoration

The construction of large water infrastructure projects in the early 20th century contributed substantially to the evolution of life in the arid West. The process of gaining approval for reconstructing Arrowrock Dam in the 21st century has become a game of political chess. The last major flood over 9,800 cubic feet per second occurred in 1983 and challenged the capacity of Arrowrock Dam to control major floods. Both federal

and state agencies knew there were limitations with Arrowrock Dam, which is an integral component of the upper Boise (Water) Project.

Federal and state government agencies later came together to address the issues with the dam. In 1992, Idaho adopted new protections of the Boise River's South, North, and Middle Forks into its state water plan. By 2004, federal agencies had completed a $20 million upgrade on the century-old ensign valves with new stainless steel clamshell gates to increase Arrowrock's ability to release high snowmelts during the yearly spring runoff. The evaluations that followed led the state to move forward on investigations of future water needs with state legislation allocating funding to survey potential water storage expansion of 12 dam sites throughout Idaho in collaboration with a federal partner starting in 2006. An agreement between the Idaho Water Resource Board and the

South Fork of the Boise River

U.S. Army Corps of Engineers locked in federal funding via the 2007 amended version of the Water Resources Development Act of 1999, which then included water supply surveying and ecosystem restoration analysis.

Arrowrock Dam appears as an example in a 2008 congressional report highlighting the need to address rising maintenance expenditures of aging federal dams. The report specifically referred to the $20 million upgrade, signifying it would not be the last upgrade as the dam completes a century of continual service. Furthermore, the succession of evaluations by the federal and state partnership ended in 2010 and placed Arrowrock Dam at the top of the list for feasibility of water storage and flood control benefits. By 2011, the Corps of Engineers was focusing specifically on Arrowrock and had presented results of a preliminary evaluation to the public for commentary on alternatives, including (1) raising the height of the dam by up to 74 feet, (2) building a new dam, (3) upgrading bridge heights downriver, and (4) replacing smaller push-up dams with inflatable weirs, among other options. Comments from community residents, governmental entities, the private sector, and environmental groups reflect a broad range of concerns, including lack of water availability, dam reconstruction, and the environmental consequences of the construction and operation.

The ecosystem restoration component in the amended Water Resources Development Act of 2007 no longer exists. Ellen Berggren, Snake River project manager at the U.S. Army Corps of Engineers, stated that funding is not available on behalf of the corps or the Idaho Water Resource Board. She added that the corps would welcome an external partner to help fund the ecological restoration effort, but that would assume familiarity with one of the most difficult valuation processes in environmental economics—that is, determining the value of impaired ecological systems. Liz Paul, the Boise River Campaign coordinator for Idaho Rivers United, said that Idaho Rivers United is willing to collaborate in restoration, but she offered little detail as to what such a partnership would accomplish. Ecosystem restoration, by definition, aims to repair damaged or destroyed ecosystems by facilitating an increase in biodiversity and balance with human systems.

Idaho Rivers United questions environmental costs of enlarging big dams.

That said, coming up with a price to realize the goal of restoration is not simple: the challenge lies in justifying the investment of tax dollars in environmental restoration of Arrowrock Dam, a site that does not directly pose negative effects on human health. The relative value would reflect a wide range of responses by Boise Valley residents to the value of higher biodiversity, which illustrates the complexity of the situation. The crux of the problem for conservationists is that the safety of certain water levels for people depends on where residential homes are built, that methods for predicting future floods are imperfect, and that residential developers driven by profit will build anywhere, even in the floodplain. Idaho Rivers United must surf these uncertainties to receive money to advocate for wise flood control, protection of the upper rivers, and provision of recreation on the Boise River. The unpredictable value attributed to the environment will make even the most ambitious environmental advocates scratch their heads when it comes to deploying an effective strategy to fund and restore the damaged reservoir ecosystems.

The Lucky Peak "rooster tail" is excess water used for power generation that comes through the dam's outlet slide gates, nicknamed "flip buckets." The release creates a huge plume of water that can reach a height of 150 feet.

Originally built for irrigation, Arrowrock Dam elicits concerns that convey a provocative shift in construction justification. A clear decline in acres of farmland to subdivision housing in the riverside communities in the Boise Valley trumpet serious flood risks. Changes in land use make irrigation storage and flood protection of an ever-growing urban population on the river's floodplain a formidable opponent of environmental protection. Likewise, the water management mission of the U.S. Bureau of Reclamation and the flood control mission of the U.S. Army Corps of Engineers align with the interests of the most powerful stakeholders in the valley below the dam: canal companies and farmers with "first-in-time" water rights are well established and have plenty of political connections within the area. Naturally, when an opportunity to expand water supply comes about, they are all ears. The maximum 74-foot dam-raising option would amplify the storage capacity of Arrowrock Reservoir by an additional 300,000 acre-feet.

In a February 4, 2014, *Idaho Statesman* article, environmental journalist Rocky Barker wrote that the maximum number of acre-feet proposed by the Corps of Engineers might seem substantial, but after current irrigators take their share, only 60,000 acre-feet will remain for distribution. In addition, COMPASS (Commmunity Planning Association of Southwest Idaho) projects that the Boise metropolitan area will reach a population of 1.5 million by 2040. These projections are at the core of the Idaho Water Resource Board's argument to move forward with the expanded dam; an increased need for water for a growing Boise Valley population warrants state action.

Historic Arrowrock

As all rivers do, the Boise River experiences cycles of flooding caused by melting of the snowpack in the high mountains above the city. The water infrastructure and development have long since domesticated the Boise River. Dam construction and active river channelization were responses to the flooding, which, in turn, permitted the transformation of the floodplain into urban developments. The living river soon was vanquished as dam construction and enhanced flood protection became normal practices. This security, provided by four major dams—Diversion in 1908, Arrowrock in 1915, Anderson Ranch in 1941, and Lucky Peak in 1955—bolstered growth on the more susceptible tracts of land in the valley.

Prior to the completion of the Arrowrock Dam, irrigation and flood control systems in the Boise Valley limited development on the floodplain to farming. Valley residents understood that building houses or any other physical structures on the floodplain guaranteed damage from the

Construction of Arrowrock Dam

annual snowmelt. The high costs and low returns of building a dam on the Boise River detoured private companies from domesticating the river via the federal land exchange with private companies granted by the Carey Act of 1894, which proved successful in the Magic Valley just over 100 miles southeast of the Boise Valley. The funding necessary for the project came after passage of the Reclamation Act of 1902, when farmers petitioned the federal government to build a federally funded dam for the benefit of irrigation.

Construction camp in Arrowrock Canyon, about 1914

The U.S. Army Corps of Engineers conducted the initial reconnaissance surveys around the existing location of the Arrowrock Dam from 1903 to 1904 on behalf of the U.S. Reclamation Service (now the U.S. Bureau of Reclamation). Congressional approval for funding the project came on June 10, 1910. Construction on the selected site did not officially begin until many preliminary projects were completed, including putting in a 17-mile rail line, a sawmill, a camp fit to house 1,500 men, a 1,500-kilowatt power plant for concrete mixers, and 54 miles of telephone line laid for direct contact with the main Boise Reclamation Service office. Furthermore, two cofferdams and a diversion tunnel were built before official construction began in 1911. The dam cost approximately $5 million and provided 276,500 acre-feet of water until 1937, when the Corps of Engineers added an additional 5 feet to the height of the dam.

Environmental Matters

Unlike during the initial construction, the current decision-making process pits Idaho Rivers United directly against the Arrowrock project. Idaho Rivers United defends the state river protections, the federal Endangered Species Act, and the National Environmental Protection Act, and it claims that raising Arrowrock Dam would waste tax dollars. Paul stresses her point that "there is absolutely no good reason to raise the Arrowrock Dam." She adds that the Treasure Valley has plenty of water and that people "need to have better water use practices instead of spending millions of dollars on a project that will inevitably benefit only the people living on the floodplain."

Idaho Rivers United focuses on the potential alternatives to flood control, such as forming off-stream detention ponds, raising bridges, building levees, creating better construction zoning on the river's floodplain, and improving water conservation standards. "Investing in such alternatives would save taxpayers thousands if not millions of dollars in comparison to building a dam," Paul said. With tight budgets on both sides of the state and federal partnership, these measures should hold some appeal. However, the ideas proposed by Idaho Rivers United forgo the economic realities of setting aside land for such flood control runoff and the water storage ambitions of the state. Private citizens own 75% of the land in the river's floodplain. In competition with developers, the market prices and cost to purchase enough land for those measures could be an expensive endeavor. Despite making the valid points of demanding water conservation and the inherently unequal benefits that would result from raising the dam, the Idaho Rivers United position relies heavily on the provisions set by federal and state protections of the North and Middle Forks of the Boise River.

Raising and rebuilding Arrowrock Dam would occur on the west side of the dam, below and immediately beside

Gravel removal helps control water flow on the Boise River.

the existing reservoir. Idaho's protection statutes specifically exclude construction or expansion of dams or impoundments, construction of hydropower projects, construction of water diversion works, dredge or placer mining, alterations of the streambed, and mineral, sand, or gravel extraction within the streambed in a protected river. Because the rebuilt dam would be below the protected river, it could be permitted. However, federal and state laws protect bull trout as an endangered species, and bull trout live in and above Arrowrock Reservoir. The state also protects the wild, recreational, and scenic river above the reservoir. If the dam were raised 74 feet, the reservoir would inundate a portion of the protected river within the Middle and South Forks of the Boise River. If the state law remains intact, Idaho Rivers United could be the sure winner, but keeping the law intact might be a big challenge in the conservative state of Idaho.

Bull trout migrate to spawn.

The impending problem remains in the expansion of Arrowrock Reservoir and the construction of new access roads. The Corps of Engineers estimates a maximum expansion of 6.5 miles to the reservoir if a 74-foot dam raising occurs. The U.S. Fish and Wildlife Service states that any "activities" above normal high water marks "can and often do impact critical habitat areas." Such activities include the maintenance or building of roads. Therefore, one of the primary issues with the project will be in the environmental impact statement required under the National Environmental Protection Act.

This statement will include the expansion of the reservoir that would inundate roads, creeks, and other land below the new proposed 3,290-foot water mark.

These activities have the potential to conflict with the Endangered Species Act, which states that federal agencies must "insure [sic] that any [federal] action authorized, funded, or carried out by such agency is not likely to jeopardize the continued existence of any endangered species or threatened species or result in the destruction or adverse modification of [critical] habitat." However, section 7(h) of the Endangered Species Act also states that if an action clearly outweighs the alternatives that may conserve critical habitat, an exemption to the law is possible. The action must be in the public interest, it must have a regional or national significance, and a biological assessment must be prepared to determine the adverse effects of the proposed action. The governor of Idaho can apply for an exemption to alter the designated critical habitat. The outcome of the biological assessment and other political factors would then be judged by a federal committee, nicknamed "the God Committee," that would recommend a decision on the governor's request for the exemption.

Arrowrock Dam was once the tallest in the world, but it may not be enough to prevent flood risk.

The effects of expanding the reservoir on the tributaries closest to the main body of Arrowrock Reservoir will most likely be the key issue for Idaho Rivers United. Furthermore, the politically conservative Idaho Water Resource Board holds the power to modify the state protections to move forward with their plans for water storage. However, turning back the protected rivers law will create an uproar in the state of Idaho and in the changing Congress.

Urban Growth and Flood Risk

Ellen Berggren of the Corps of Engineers asserts that the Boise Valley has never been without flood risk, and addressing flood risk is an integral part of the corps's mission. Berggren says it is difficult to get the funding approval from Congress for direct flood control measures, which stifles efforts by the Walla Walla District Corps. Valley residents have constantly battled with flooding throughout the Boise River's recorded history. The book *When the River Rises* offers one of the best summaries of that history. The title alone asserts the reality of a living river. Author Susan Stacy describes major flood events from 1943 to 1985. The 1943 flood event caused an estimated $1 million in damages and solidified the decision to build Lucky Peak Dam. Despite the flooding certainties that continued over the years, it was ultimately pressure from irrigators, and not the flooding itself, that drove most of the policy decisions pertaining to dam building.

The second major flood events, in 1983 and 1985, truly tested the Boise Project dams. The winter snowmelt uncovered the limitations of the Arrowrock Dam specifically. The timeworn ensign valves that released excess water during the 1985 spring melt created a noticeable bottleneck. Thus, the upgrade on the Arrowrock made for more than just routine maintenance. In 1915, engineers did not incorporate or even understand the precaution of building dams to withstand the modern standard of a "probable maximum flood." Despite the new improvements to Arrowrock Dam, the Idaho Flood and Seismic Risk Portfolio of 2012-2017 ranks the lower Boise River sub-basin as the number one area of concern in the state because of population growth on the floodplain.

Overall growth in the Boise Valley has received national attention. An article in *USA Today*, titled "No End in Sight for Idaho's Growth," describes the ongoing trend. The article boasts of economic prosperity and urban expansion, specifically in the Treasure Valley just prior to the nation's economic downturn. Even in the shadow of the 2008 economic crisis, an unrelenting push for riverside development continues. Remarkably, some of the most expensive pieces of property in the valley lie in the most volatile places geographically, including the 952 homes under federal flood protection insurance directly on the floodplain. Well-known hazards have yet to detour economic gains by developers who use aesthetics as a selling point.

Nowhere will the potential for future floodplain development be greater than in the cities of Star, Eagle, and the western edges of Garden City. These cities hold some of the remaining floodplain farmland in the Boise metro area. According to the U.S. Department of Agriculture's census, the housing boom from 2002 to 2007 reduced Ada County's farmland by 14% and by 4% in adjacent Canyon County. Records from 2012 show that only 16% of the total area in the two counties qualifies as irrigated farmland.

Agricultural land is perfect for developers because the land is typically flat and free of debris, which makes construction that much easier. Aerial images of the valley demonstrate the expanses of land between Eagle and Star as ripe for the picking for subdivision contractors. Growth seems to be an inescapable part of any thriving city, but the laissez-faire floodplain zoning that has taken place over the past 50 years highlights the lucrative profits and apparent risks involved. In addition, COMPASS has been working since 2002 to build a commuter transit expansion on State Street that would facilitate the flow of traffic from downtown Boise through Eagle to Star. If such a design were to be implemented, the farmland and riparian regions on the northern banks of the Boise River between Eagle and Star would eventually sell at premium rates.

The proposal for construction at Arrowrock Dam influences all valley residents, but canal companies, farmers, floodplain homeowners, and the defenders of the river's health stand to be the most affected. Agencies involved in the matter begin with the U.S. Bureau of Reclamation, which rightfully owns Arrowrock Dam and whose core mission in the arid West is water storage. The bureau has operated the largest water storage facilities in the Boise Valley since the completion of Diversion Dam in 1909. Historically, the efforts of the corps and the bureau transformed ideas into reality by constructing all stages of the Boise Project. Officials at the Walla Walla District Army Corps of Engineers are concerned about flood protection of the largest population in their region. Modifying dams to accommodate for the "probable maximum flood risk" is a part of water resource management that would avoid difficult decision making, leaving principal agencies liable for damages. The potential economic losses in property damages are a concern to the federal government if payouts under the National Flood Insurance Program are significant.

Taking a stroll on the greenbelt in the cities of Boise, Garden City, and Eagle confirms the volume of properties directly on the floodplain of the Boise River and its tributaries. The three cities are participants in the National Flood Insurance Program. The program is not a requirement, but it allows for variable subsidy rates of insurance for city residents who meet or exceed federal emergency management standards. As of 2012, the liability in the lower Boise River sub-basin totaled $462 million with a collection of $1.1 million in total premiums by the federal government.

The Boise River floods at Glenwood Bridge, 2006.

Subsidies are available for residents on a scale that rates cities from 1 to 10, 1 being the highest in terms of the city's flood protection efforts and 10 meaning that the city does not participate in the program. Boise and Eagle have a rating of 6 and Garden City a rating of 8. The active performance on flooding awareness and flood risk prevention standards gives these cities their ratings. A set of 19 individual measures are split into four categories: public information about risks, mapping and regulations, flood damage reduction, and warning/response. Despite the implementation of some standards in these cities, the risk still exists, as they have continued to experience flooding events. For example, 1998 flooding in Eagle affected multiple subdivisions, led to the evacuation of 60 residents, and caused significant damage to a section of the Boise River Greenbelt. But in 2006, the flooding of unfinished Laguna Pointe subdivision on Eagle Island did not stop the contractor from selling the homes to the present residents.

Most urban development on the river's floodplain is inhabited by affluent property owners who would benefit from flood control measures. These costly properties stretch from below the Diversion Dam to above the city of Eagle. Garden City serves as an exception in that sections of its riverside property consist of lower income neighborhoods. However, the city's newly established urban renewal agency hopes to change this with a bulk of their projects focusing on riverside developments. The most recent of these projects, the River Front East Urban Renewal Plan, aims to convert a 199-acre plot along the Boise River into high-priced housing, which will expand the Waterfront District subdivision built in 2008. The redevelopment will remove the present lower income trailer homes on the river's edge and give the area a modern condominium-style facelift.

Riverfront homes dot the Boise River.

On the north side of the river, Boise also works toward reclaiming underdeveloped riverfront areas. The Environmental Protection Agency's brownfields project in the west downtown area off 30th Street is one example. The site of an oil storage facility from 1920 to 2009, the land is known for its soil contamination but is now under consideration for urban renewal. These are just a few examples of cities in the valley planning around a reliably tamed Boise River. As projections for the future linger, many of the alternatives, such as retention ponds, are at odds with real estate investors funding projects throughout the valley. Assuming regulations for floodplain construction do not change, the potential economic profits from new developments on the river's floodplain are too lucrative to allow no construction.

The Future of Arrowrock Dam

The economic advantages that may come from raising Arrowrock Dam can equate to variable gains distributed throughout the Boise Valley beyond that of property values. The water expansion to the proposed 300,000 acre-feet could provide, at current water bank rates ($17), a maximum value of $5.1 million. With the state's general fund for the fiscal year of 2015 approximating $2.9 billion, the number may sound like a drop in the bucket. However, when Arrowrock Dam underwent its $20 million upgrade in 2004, the federal government anticipated a return of only $6.9 million over a 15-year period from the State of Idaho. Berggren stated that the typical cost share between state and federal agencies ranges

Spring floods and summer droughts drive the politics of Arrowrock Dam.

from a 30/70 to 40/60 split, respectively. The purchase of a new dam at this discount may be worth it for some, but the actual price tag of the proposed dam remains to be determined if the project is approved.

The contention among the irrigators, developers, riverside residents, and environmental advocates involved in the potential raising of Arrowrock makes the process an attention-grabbing dilemma for the valley. The push for flood control by the U.S. Army Corps of Engineers works for the floodplain residents and developers. The Idaho Water Resource Board wishes for more water storage, which serves the irrigators and the U.S. Bureau of Reclamation. Idaho Rivers United and many existing residents along the river want protection and greater consideration of the health of the South, Middle, and North Forks of the Boise River. All the interests converging at once will make the final decision a very difficult one. The corps hopes to have an environmental impact statement by the end of 2015 and final recommendation by 2017. That assumes that all goes well. Depending on the outcome of the environmental impact statement, Idaho Rivers United may decide to challenge the findings in the assessment. This may lead to lawsuits that would further delay the process of deciding whether or not to begin construction.

The next few years will prove whether the value of ecosystem services can stand against floodplain development plans and future water demands. Whatever the conclusion of the proposal, the topics of water availability, flood control, and ecosystem values will continue to flow throughout the Boise Valley.

RICHARD MARTINEZ has an associate's degree in biology from the College of Southern Idaho and a bachelor's degree in environmental studies from Boise State University, with minors in geospatial analysis and sustainability. He was a McNair Scholar.

3 | Earth, Water, and Gender

Two great American writers tell parallel stories of conquest.

by Erin Nelson

The building of the Boise River framed the story of nature's conquest in a classic novel about engineering and gender in the pioneer West. Wallace Stegner's *Angle of Repose* (published in 1971)—the title itself taken from the work of Mary Hallock Foote—fictionalized the lives of Boise settlers Arthur De Wint Foote and Mary Hallock Foote, who arrived in 1884 to begin the Boise River irrigation project. Mary Hallock Foote, a talented illustrator and writer, recorded their time spent on the Boise River in great detail through letters, drawings, and prose. Stegner appropriated letters from Mary Hallock Foote to write *Angle of Repose*, and this decision remains controversial among literary scholars today.

Stegner has been hailed as a "western humanist" and praised for his ability to encapsulate regional history and authentic life on the frontier. Much of this praise accumulated after the publication of *Angle of Repose*. Stegner claimed to have permission to use Hallock Foote's letters, which were published a year after Stegner's novel in a volume titled *A Victorian Gentlewoman in the Far West*. Members of the Foote family stipulated that Stegner hide the source of the letters, and so Stegner refrained from crediting Mary Hallock Foote as a source. Some descendants of the Foote family objected to the great liberties Stegner took with using Mary Hallock Foote's writing, but Stegner maintained that he was following the family's wishes. The story of Mary Hallock Foote still arises in literary discourse about the blurred lines between memoir and fiction. Arthur Foote and Mary Hallock Foote remain formative parts of Idaho history and the history of the Boise River to this day, with controversy circulating around Stegner's use of Mary Hallock Foote's letters and Arthur Foote's attempt to construct the Boise River irrigation project.

Arthur De Wint Foote was born in 1849 in Guilford, Connecticut. He was close to graduating from Yale College's Sheffield Scientific School when he left, in 1868, to begin his career in construction and business ventures. Foote's pursuits eventually led to his career in civil engineering. Foote was an advocate for the expansion of the New West,

and this belief system motivated Arthur Foote and his wife, Mary, to move to Boise, Idaho, where they settled along the Boise River. Arthur Foote bought the water rights on the Boise River where he designed the Boise River irrigation project. The Footes stayed in Boise for 12 years while the project developed until it failed due to lack of funding. The family then moved to Grass Valley, California, where Arthur Foote worked as a general manager of the North Star Mine. There, he and his wife

Illustration depicting the pioneer life of Mary and Arthur Foote.

built the North Star House in 1905, which is also known as Foote Mansion. Foote Mansion became an important setting in *Angle of Repose*, personifying the trend of "western elegance" that the Footes embraced and perpetuated in the West.

Wallace Stegner, Mary Hallock Foote, and a Literary Controversy

While Arthur Foote focused on his goals of westward expansion, his wife, Mary Hallock Foote, kept valuable documentation and meticulous recordings of her travels with Arthur. These documents comprise some of the most prized encapsulations of life in Boise. Mary Hallock was born in 1847 in Milton, New York, to a Quaker family. She studied at the Female Collegiate Seminary in Poughkeepsie, New York, and attended the Cooper Institute School of Design for Women, one of the rare institutions dedicated to educating women at the time. By her early 20s, Hallock had established herself as a reputable illustrator and artist. After marrying Arthur Foote in 1876, Mary Hallock Foote was less than enthusiastic about leaving the East, but she became inspired by the philosophy of the New West. While traveling westward, and after having settled in the West, she recorded her impressions in writings and drawings, which were published in *Century Magazine* and other newspapers and literary journals of the time.

Wallace Stegner's *Angle of Repose* won the Pulitzer Prize for fiction in 1972.

A formal yet sociable person, Hallock Foote befriended her neighbors who had settled along the Boise River. These people often became characters in her stories, which she sold to newspapers and early Boise settlers. In so doing, she became the primary breadwinner of the household while Arthur tried tirelessly to fund his irrigation project. This gender role reversal was unusual for the time. Because Arthur's irrigation project had drained the family's savings—so much so that the Footes were unable to afford their rent in town—the family settled along the Boise River in a small log cabin built by Arthur.

Hallock Foote wrote novels and nonfiction stories about the West, articulating her own narrative of an eastern immigrant to the West. Although she wrote her memoir, *A Victorian Gentlewoman in the Far West: The Reminiscences of Mary Hallock Foote*, in 1924, 14 years before her death, it wasn't published until 1972. Stegner had access to the memoir long before its publication and stated that he was attracted to the manuscript, referring to Hallock Foote as one of the best storytellers and chroniclers of life in the western coal mines. Stegner even taught some of Hallock Foote's short stories in his class "The Rise of Realism" at Stanford University.

About 10% of *Angle of Repose* comes verbatim from *A Victorian Gentlewoman in the Far West*, and several passages are multiple paragraphs long. Stegner biographer Jackson

Benson cites and forgives the "38 instances of letter quotation for a total of 61 pages in a book of 555 pages." Stegner also used small quotations from Hallock Foote's writings, as well as thousands of small phrases and details found in her journals. When questioned about the liberties he took with her letters and stories, Stegner responded, "To be frank, she did not strike me as important enough historically to make her more than modestly interesting—a talented woman on the frontier. By converting her to fiction I at least had the chance to make her immortal."

Beyond this appropriation, Hallock Foote's family objected to the framing of Stegner's character Susan Ward, who was largely based on Mary Hallock Foote. Stegner bent the facts of Hallock Foote's life to fit with his fiction, portraying Susan as an unhappy wife who possibly has an affair with her husband's assistant. During the affair, Susan's young daughter drowns in the nearby river. Susan is conceited and wary of the West, which is disconcerting to the Foote family and fans of Mary Hallock Foote. As they understand it, Stegner used Hallock Foote's writing to ultimately criticize and slander the real woman. Stegner's use of her work spurs further questions: If Hallock Foote's work had been as well known as it is today, would Stegner have been forced to credit her with his use of her life and words? If Hallock Foote had been a man, would her relatives and fans have taken her life more seriously and, as a result, taken more ownership of her work? If Stegner wasn't such an established literary figure, would he have been challenged more to divulge the source of his "inspiration"?

Susan's strained marriage with her husband, Lyman Ward, is a major conflict in *Angle of Repose*, and much of this tension was based on Mary Hallock Foote's difficult marriage to Arthur Foote. Mary's experiences with her troubled marriage to Arthur and her adjustments to life in the West became meaningful examples of imperfect unions that emerge in the novel. In her article "A Sympathetic Misunderstanding? Mary Hallock Foote's Mining West," Janet Floyd wrote, "It is ... probable to argue that Foote's class and gender allowed her a particular kind of experience in the West—one characterized by detachment, perhaps, but not one wholly organized by oppositions of East and West, or by positions of alienation and tentative assimilation."

This unique experience of the West helped Mary Hallock Foote crystallize her mixed emotions about Boise in her fiction and nonfiction. She was far enough removed from western culture to be an acute observer, yet she was fascinated with the people and used her artistic talents to portray life on the Boise River. Hallock Foote wrote some of her most significant fiction during her time in Boise from 1884 to 1895, despite her sense of loneliness and isolation. In addition, she completed some of her most famous illustrations, including "The Irrigation Ditch" and "Afternoon at a Ranch," while in Boise. These illustrations depict life on the Boise River in ways that suggest that Hallock Foote felt a strange mixture of isolation and fascination with the area, noting that the men who populated the area did not have families and merely inhabited the land to work.

Hallock Foote wrote five novels while in Boise, titled *John Bodewin's Testimony* (1886), *The Last Assembly Ball* (1889), *The Chosen Valley* (1892), *Coeur d'Alene* (1894), and *In Exile and Other Stories* (1894). *The Chosen Valley*, notably, told the story of the building of a dam in the Snake River Valley, and *Coeur d'Alene* portrayed the struggle between miners and mine owners in northern Idaho. Many of these stories were inspired by her real-life knowledge of Arthur's involvement with expanding mining in the West. Mary often incorporated the people she met through Arthur's employment into her stories, basing her characters on the authentic experiences of her friends and community. This writing style has ironically been compared with Stegner's style of using real stories as a scaffold for his fiction.

While Mary Foote adjusted to life in the West, Arthur Foote dedicated time to developing the Boise River irrigation project, which aimed to build dams and canals on the Boise River that would bring water to desert farms that struggled to obtain proper irrigation. Although Arthur was a good engineer, he was a poor businessman. Arthur was often naive

"The Irrigation Ditch"

and optimistic with his investors, trusting men who would invest their money in the project and then suddenly withdraw their funds. Despite this struggle, he remained dedicated to his project for 12 years, putting his family in financial strain. The Boise River irrigation project eventually failed, and the Foote family left Boise to chase other civil engineering pursuits in California. Despite Arthur's failure, his work helped inspire the Arrowrock Dam project that developed 25 years after the Footes had left Boise. The Arrowrock Dam project was the most ambitious and significant canal project to date for the United States Reclamation Service.

Footes' Canyon House on the Boise River

The Canyon House was designed and built by Arthur De Wint Foote in 1885, using funds from literary works by his wife, Mary Hallock Foote.

In 2015, the remnants of the Canyon House built by the Footes sit 12.5 miles east of the Boise city center at the confluence of Lydle Gulch and the Boise River, on top of a small knoll on the south band of the gulch. The curve of the Boise River rests just 40 meters from the rubble, and a fenced-off square of basalt stone foundation marks the spot where the Foote house once stood. A hand-built wooden fence, the vague outline of the Foote house's foundation, and a plaque dedicated to the Foote family are all that remain of the once-historic house on the hill.

Arthur and Mary Foote settled along the Boise River in 1885. Mary's novel, *John Bodewin's Testimony*, was the family's sole source of income after Arthur encountered financial problems with the Boise River irrigation project. The money Mary made from the sale of the novel paid for the construction of the Foote house. Arthur designed the house and began construction using organic materials from the site. Mary documented the process, writing that Arthur used "materials at hand, with walls two feet thick, of the rough basalt rock, using mud for mortar and for plastering the interior walls and partitions." She also wrote, "We began to realize that we should need a house if we spent the winter in the Canyon. ... A. was the architect and made his choice of material on the spot, those wasted rockslides only a short haul from the hill where we chalked out our ground plan."

Arthur wished to be close to the river so he could easily complete irrigation projects in the area. Mary, however, was hesitant to leave the city and considered the rural area desolate and remote. Mary wrote in a letter to her best friend Helena, "There is something terribly sobering about these solitudes, these waste places of earth. They belittle everything one is or tries to do. ... Very few things in art hold their own against it." She often longed for the culture and people back East, but she was drawn to the West and its rural landscape. Mary also revealed that an important reason for living outside Boise was to keep the Foote children "away from the commonness of the Boise atmosphere." Mary, a Victorian cosmopolitan lady of New York City, eventually fell in love with the western setting of the Boise River, adapting her experiences into much of the content that became Stegner's *Angle of Repose*.

"Engineer's Mate" depicts Mary Hallock Foote's arrival in Kuna en route to Boise.

The house was modest, but Arthur's careful planning and hard work resulted in a small but homey space for the Foote family to inhabit. In her poem, "Mary Hallock Foote at Stone House," she wrote, "With corner pillars rooted in the hill/And sloping roof extending its round crown,/Your home seems grown out of the knoll."

The site housed Mary and Arthur Foote, their three children, a governess, a cook, a nurse, and an engineer. Arthur modeled the house after the modern bungalow at the time, featuring built-in furniture that was unusual in design and Japanese prints installed on the walls of the dining room. The architecture and unique design signified that the Footes had

Mary Hallock Foote drew scenes of pioneer life in Idaho. "A Pretty Girl in the West," Canyon House veranda, circa 1890.

artistic and unusual taste for the region. Mary created several illustrations of the surrounding wilderness during the 10 years the family spent on the Boise River, and cartographers used the illustrations as references while mapping and studying the area years later.

Once settled along the Boise River, Hallock Foote continued to write and illustrate, creating pieces of fiction based on her neighbors and townspeople. She sketched people and landscapes along the river, publishing many of her articles in *Century Magazine*. About her home in the Boise Canyon, she wrote: "That V-shape in the notch where the river went out and the sunset looked in bounded our world toward the valley; the bend in the river above us where the hills interlocked shut us off in that direction." When the family left the home to move to California, she remarked, "Of all our wild nest building, this was the wildest and most improvident and hardest to leave."

Stegner, Western Irrigation, and the Boise River

While Stegner is at the center of much controversy surrounding *Angle of Repose*, one thing he and Mary Hallock Foote had in common was their love of the American West. Stegner commented extensively in the novel about the influence of western life on the Boise River. As the land became more populated and irrigated, the landscape began to suffer. Urban growth created a demand for more water, and expansion in the West compounded the problem because of the land's aridity. Westerners relied on a high-tech hydraulic society to supply water, which countered the philosophy of the New West that drove people to go west, claim their land, and live without limitations to freedom. The more the West expanded, the more citizens had to depend on governmentally or corporately supplied water from irrigation projects.

As a result of his exposure to the American West in early childhood, Stegner was knowledgeable about the environment. Stegner was born in Iowa in 1909 and moved to North Dakota, Washington State, and then to Eastend, Saskatchewan. His father, George Stegner, was what Stegner later called a "boomer," a man looking to find fortune in the West and who, not finding it in one place, moved to another. George relentlessly pursued this dream of American prosperity, moving his family to the Saskatchewan-Montana border.

Author Wallace Stegner

Stegner's fascination with the aridity of the West began in his early childhood on the homestead. The Stegners grew wheat, which required summer rain to grow, but the dryness of the land caused the crops to dust out. Stegner's mother longed to stay in one place, and she was grateful the family moved to Eastend to farm for many years. The *Angle of Repose* character Susan Burling Ward is similar to Stegner's mother in the sense that she attempted to find a home and community wherever she moved. Stegner's mother, as he put it, was "always hopefully, hopelessly trying to nest" in all the places around the West the family moved during Stegner's adolescence. This period in Eastend was the only time in Stegner's life that his family was together in one place, and leaving Saskatchewan was difficult.

After failing to grow crops in Saskatchewan, Stegner's family moved to Great Falls, Salt Lake City, Hollywood, Reno, and various other places. This transient time was similar to the lives of the traveling Foote family, and in many ways, Stegner could relate to the Footes' conflicted feelings about western culture. "Between my twelfth and twenty-first years we must have lived in twenty different houses," Stegner admitted in his autobiographical collection of essays, *Where the Bluebird Sings to the Lemonade Springs*. He continued, "[We] tried to make country and climate over to fit our existing habits and desires. Instead of listening to the silence, we have shouted into the void."

Stegner became fascinated by the aridity of the West, and much of his inner conflict about western expansion is channeled through the character Oliver Ward, who attempts to irrigate the Boise River in *Angle of Repose*. Oliver Ward is a bright, straightforward, and honest man who moves all over the West following different jobs. He is a mining engineer and has lived in Colorado, California, New Mexico, and Idaho, taking his family with him with nearly every move. This results in the family settling in some strange homes "in the wildest of places." Oliver's honesty often limits his ability to achieve his goals—like Arthur Foote, he is cheated out of investment deals with his irrigation projects and often places too much faith in sly businessmen who run the family into bankruptcy.

Oliver is determined to bring water to the West, assuming it is the "Eden" the New West myth proclaims it to be, by embarking on the Boise River irrigation project. Oliver's unsuccessful attempt to dominate the river is an example of Stegner's belief that landscape has the powerful ability to shape humanity, despite our wholehearted attempts to shape the land. Stegner states people in the West "have never stayed in one place long enough to learn it, or have learned it only to leave it." This idea is personified in Oliver, who naively fails to learn the land and then fails to alter it.

Steger states in his part-memoir, part-fiction novel *Wolf Willow* that "short of living it out, no system of farming, no matter how strenuously applied, could produce crops in that country during one of the irregular and unpredictable periods of drought." Much like Arthur Foote, Oliver Ward refused to give up his project because he believed that irrigation would be the next greatest movement of the West. He eventually drives the family into financial ruin, fighting to remake the landscape into one that can produce the crops Stegner argued can't exist in the region.

Stegner was most entrenched in commentary on western culture regarding the exploitation of water resources. In a place like Boise, we remake the landscapes we love, creating conflict between private and public spheres, the natural and the unnatural, and the idea that water is owned by the community and should be managed for the public's welfare. He asserted that the arid environment of the West enabled the worst and most disastrous pillaging of local resources, with rivers and aquifers suffering the most. In *Where the Bluebird Sings*, he wrote that western settlers "came to pillage, or work for pillagers, rather than to settle for life. When the pillaging was done or the dream exploded, they moved on, to be replaced in the next boom by others just as hopeful and just as footloose." Stegner asserted that westerners carve out canals and levees to prove they are the masters of nature, but western rivers eventually mute those dreams and reclaim their own paths.

A reclamation engineer stands beneath Arthur Foote's ambition about a mile below the family homestead, 1907.

Fredrik Christian Brøgger claims in his essay, "Wallace Stegner and the Western Environment: Hydraulics, Placelessness, and (Lack of) Identity," that "Stegner's ultimate point in *Where the Bluebird Sings* is that human societies and cultures will remain vigorous and dynamic only to the extent that they are able to adapt themselves to their environment." This, in many senses, rings true throughout *Angle of Repose* as well. Susan Burling Ward struggles to adapt to the new harshness of her surroundings, instead finding solace in her writing, artwork, and possible affair. Her young daughter, Agnes, succumbs to the dangers of the West and tragically drowns in the river. Oliver attempts to dominate the Boise

River and alter the landscape, only to find out that it ultimately shapes him. Mary Hallock Foote wrote about the real-life irrigation failure, "There it was finished—the last of our dreams in Idaho … the small but mighty work of man and the vast overpowering Nature to be used and controlled. … What insolence—what a gesture!"

Often, Mary Hallock Foote and Stegner complement and contrast each other in their works. Stegner, a noted conservationist, advocated for water preservation and remarked that "in the dry West, using water means using it *up*." Hallock Foote, however, arrived in the West at a time when the West was still a mystery and conservation was second to western expansion. She wrote several passages about how excited she was for Arthur's new business venture in Boise, not knowing the future ramifications of irrigation on the landscape.

A Complicated Narrative

The relationship between Wallace Stegner, the Footes, and the Boise River will always remain complicated. Their narratives both bleed into and contradict each other, much like the Boise River itself. History is always a narrative told from a specific perspective, and Stegner and Hallock Foote speak together, arguing with each other and shaping each other. What is clear is that both Stegner and Hallock Foote wrote about a beautiful land overcome by humanity's desire to control and irrigate. Stegner clearly and vocally advocated preservation and environmentalism. Hallock Foote lived in an era before the West was fully explored. She and her husband Arthur were part of a generation that sought to harness and shape the land, sometimes successfully, sometimes unsuccessfully. Today, Hallock Foote's reflections on the Boise River, life in the West, and the arid landscape of Boise, Idaho, remain some of the most important encapsulations of life on the Boise frontier.

Some scholars believe that Hallock Foote was largely forgotten by the time of her death in 1938 and that Stegner revitalized her by incorporating her work into his novel *Angle of Repose*. Hallock Foote's words, however, make it clear that she does not need Stegner to resuscitate, immortalize, or validate her work or to explain to readers the beauty of the Boise River Valley where she made her home. In *The Last Assembly Ball, and the Fate of a Voice*, she speaks forever for herself: "There are many loose pages of the earth's history scattered through the unpeopled regions of the Far West. ... An ancient lava stream once submerged the valley. Its hardening crust, bursting asunder in places, left great crooked rents through which the subsequent drainage from the mountain slopes found a way down to the desert plains. In one of these furrows, left by the fiery plowshare, a river, now called the Wallula, made its bed. Hurling itself from side to side scouring out its straitened boundaries with tons of sand torn from the mountains, it slowly widened and deepened, and wore its ancient channel into the canyon. ... Along the bluffs, the basalt walls are reared in tiers of columns with hexagonal cleavage. ... A column or a group of columns becomes dislocated from the mass, rests so slightly apart ... it topples down; the jointed columns fall apart, and their fragments go to increase the heap of debris which has found its angle of repose at the foot of the cliff."

An engraved portrait of Mary Hallock Foote, about 1888

ERIN NELSON is a Boise-based writer and event coordinator for Rediscovered Books in downtown Boise. She enjoys reading obsessively, studying gender issues, playing Galaga, and napping with her cat.

4 | Float, Paddle, and Surf

River sports make a tourist attraction.

by Travis Armstrong

Whitewater kayakers and surfers cut, rolled, flipped, and performed other feats of skill while riding the fast moving wave at the Boise River Park. The spectators standing along the river's edge gathered not only to watch and admire the athleticism of the participants but also to appreciate and celebrate the recently constructed Harry Morrison Dam. The inaugural Boise River Park Surf and Kayak Rally, held in June 2014, was organized not as a competition but rather as a showcase of the new Boise River Park with the dam as its centerpiece.

The 2014 Surf and Kayak Rally marked the newest chapter in the history of river sports on the Boise River. In July 1959, the Boise chapter of the Junior Chamber of Commerce, or Jaycees, hosted the inaugural Keep Idaho Green raft race. The Jaycees organized the race to call attention to the issue of human-caused forest fires. With several hundred spectators gathered onshore, rafters paddled and battled their way down the river with many rafts capsizing en route. The *Idaho Statesman* reported, "More Boise Jaycees were dunked in the river as a result of mishaps during the four-mile run than doughnuts at a Pentagon building coffee-break."

Although separated by more than a half century, the Keep Idaho Green raft race and the Boise River Park Surf and Kayak Rally were made possible through an actively managed Boise River. Irrigators have long controlled the river, and the City of Boise has worked to make the river safer and more accessible for a wide variety of river sports enthusiasts. Rafters, tubers, kayakers, and surfers have been shaped by this management of the river and in turn have helped to shape the river themselves.

As the late historian J.M. Neil pointed out in his unpublished manuscript *City Limits*, "Until the completion of Lucky Peak Dam in 1955, the variations in river flow would have sharply limited the opportunity for tubing." The Boise River, once highly braided and with flows susceptible to both seasonal floods and summertime drought, became much more predictable once Lucky Peak Dam was built. Although the dam was built primarily to meet irrigation and safety needs, rafters and tubers capitalized

on the consistent flows. They now could float the cool river throughout the duration of Boise's long and scorching summers without fear of running aground because of low flows.

The consistent flows of the river provided by the Lucky Peak Dam would have been of little use to floaters if sanitation on the river hadn't been much improved some years prior. A *Statewide* newspaper guest editorial written in 1949 by then

Sandy Point Beach offers cold clear water for swimming at Lucky Peak State Park.

Boise Commissioner of Public Works J. V. Otter lauded the recent strides the City of Boise had made in cleaning up its river. Otter cited two major developments that had led to a far cleaner river. First, in September 1949, Boise's first sewer treatment plant came online. (Before the plant was built, raw sewage from the city flowed directly into the river.) Second, the city passed an ordinance requiring that all residential garbage be deposited in the landfill south of Boise. Before the ordinance went into place, city residents often pitched their trash in a number of unauthorized dumps, some of which were located along the river. Commissioner Otter wrote that these unauthorized dumps were a "menace to public health and ... a breeding place for rats." Without these sanitation improvements, the Keep Idaho Green raft racers would have been floating in the river along with human waste and rats scurrying along the shores.

Clayne Baker conceived the idea of the 1959 raft race. Baker, an 84-year-old Boise native, was a third-generation owner of Baker's Dairy Farm. Living a stone's throw from the Boise River to this day, Baker has long had an intimate relationship with the river. Beyond starting the annual Keep Idaho Green raft race, Baker was also an avid fly fisherman. He was a founding member of the Boise Valley Fly Fishermen's Club and he founded a popular youth fly fishing club known as the Woolly Buggers.

Competitor in the Keep Idaho Green raft race.

During the Keep Idaho Green competition, rafters launched at present-day Barber Park in east Boise and finished just west of downtown at Ann Morrison Park, which had been christened earlier that summer. Local businesses sponsored individual rafts. According to Baker, the race got "quite competitive." Spectators got into the action as well, pelting the participants with eggs and other debris. Baker smiled when recalling the event he enjoyed more than 55 years ago. He said that all "had a blast" and that the race got "kind of wild, too." There may have been some "serious drinking" going on, he admitted.

When asked about the legacy of the raft race, Baker said, "We [the Jaycees] thought that this was something that would catch on." Catch on it did. The Keep Idaho Green raft race became an annual event stretching for at least 20 summers. The well-known summertime event helped to popularize tubing on the river.

The Boise River is a popular recreation destination.

The Boise River float developed into what is now a quintessential summertime activity. On any given weekend, hordes of tubers and rafters can be seen lazily floating down the river. Ada County estimates that as many as 100,000 floats occur on the river each year. Although people can float on any section of the river, the traditional float follows the same section of the river as the Keep Idaho Green raft race. Floaters put in at Barber Park and take out at Ann Morrison Park footbridge, located a couple of hundred yards upstream from Settler's diversion dam.

Ada County manages Barber Park. As the popularity of the river float grew over the years, Ada County added amenities to match demand. Today at the park, floaters can rent tubes and rafts or inflate their own water crafts at permanent filling stations. The county built concrete fortified steps leading into the river to minimize erosion at the primary launch site.

Allen Haynes counts himself as one of the regulars on the river. For many years, he has lived in an apartment near the floater take-out at Ann Morrison Park. When the temperature

Floating the Boise River near the Baybrook Court Bridge

rises, Haynes throws his personal raft and supplies in his backpack and heads to the park. For 3 bucks he can catch a ride on an old white bus upriver to the put-in at Barber Park. School bus–style shuttles run by Epley's Whitewater leave from Ann Morrison Park on the hour during the week and every 20 minutes on the weekend. Epley's contracts with Ada County to operate both the shuttle system and the raft rentals out of Barber Park.

A nontraditional Boise State student studying to be a social worker, Haynes, now in his 50s, spends much of his free time in the summer floating the river. It is an activity that is "easy on the budget" and lets him hang out in the sun, either socializing with friends or seeking solitude and spotting wildlife, such as beavers, otters, herons, and eagles.

Haynes believes he was 12 when he first began floating the Boise River in the mid-1970s. Although not a Boise native, Haynes visited his grandparents in Boise every summer. He recalls throwing his inner tube over his shoulder and biking up to Barber Park from their house. When he was a late teenager, Haynes would hop on the back of his buddy's Honda 50 motorbike with their tubes over his shoulder and a 12-pack of beer between his legs. Back then, they would make a full day out of the trip, stopping here and there along the river to swim, lounge on a sandy beach, or build a fire for a barbeque.

Floating the river was different back then. The experience has become more controlled and regulated. With development along the river, the number of places a floater can stop and hang out along the shore has been minimized. Alcohol on the river was banned in 2005 and building a campfire is out of the question.

Stacks of rafts are ready to launch on the Boise River.

For Haynes, the changes in the river float experience are largely for the better. The population in Boise and the surrounding region skyrocketed in the past couple of decades. When he first began floating the river, he said he would see "10 to 20 other people on the river" through the course of his float. On a blistering hot summer weekend now, there are times that he is within 10 feet of other floaters for the duration of the 6-mile float. The river is packed. Haynes said that it can almost be like "a ride at some amusement park." Haynes believes floating the river in the manner that he and his friends did 30 years or more ago simply wouldn't be "safe or possible" anymore. He is happy that the river float is now more accessible for a wider variety of people.

Safety on the River

The Boise Fire Department makes the river float safer and more accessible for people like Haynes. When recreationists get into trouble on the river, the Dive and Swift Water Rescue Team goes into action. A minimum of five firefighters with advanced training geared toward water rescue are on duty at all times. The team stages their rescue boat and scuba gear out of Fire Station #1 near Fort Boise Park. Approximately 30 firefighters constitute the rescue team for the fire department.

Division Chief Paul Roberts leads the Dive and Swift Water Rescue Team. Because of the river's cold and fast moving water, Roberts states, recreating on the Boise River carries "inherent risks." In the past 5 years, the team has officially responded to 106 rescue calls. More than 90% of the calls were for swift water rescue versus encounters where scuba gear was needed.

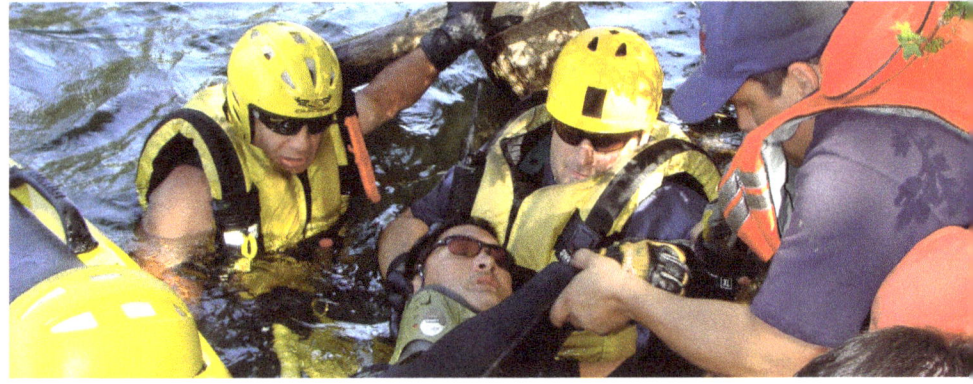

Rescue team performs life-saving techniques as part of their training.

The Boise River is rarely closed for floating. One can recreate on the river year-round. In extreme circumstances such as high flows beyond flood stage, the fire department posts closure signs on the river and sends out a public service announcement via the media. If a recreationist is rescued by the team during one of these high flow periods, that person may receive a bill from the Boise Fire Department. The bill can range from a few hundred dollars to several thousand dollars depending on the circumstances. At no other time does the rescue team bill for its services.

The team works to make the river safer in the spring before the busy recreational season ramps up for the hot summer months. The team identifies hazards in the river such as downed trees they call "sweepers." Floaters sometimes hang up on these sweepers and can get pinned under water. Regarding these hazards, the fire department consults with a variety of stakeholders that include the Idaho Fish and Game Department, Idaho Department of Water Resources, Ada County, and the City of Boise Parks and Recreation. With a consideration for fish and wildlife habitat, a mitigation plan is put together to address these hazards. The goal is to make the river safer by removing the most dangerous hazards while maintaining variety in the river flow, which is necessary for proper fish and wildlife habitat. Adhering to the mitigation plan, the rescue team, Ada County, and the City of Boise remove the identified trees and other hazards using various tools such as chainsaws from boat and shore. Once this work is completed, the fire department communicates to Ada County and other stakeholders that they have done what they can to make the river safe for the commercial phase of the float season.

Boise Fire Department team removes hazards from the waterway.

Creating a New Wave of River Sports

Now that the traditional river float through the heart of Boise was relatively safe and user friendly, the City of Boise turned its attention to the neglected section of the river west of downtown. Approximately 1 mile downriver from the floater take-out in Ann Morrison Park is the Boise River Park, a section of the river that the city has cleaned and modified to accommodate recreation for kayakers and surfers. The city opted to build the Boise River Park in two phases. Phase I of the river park entailed the rebuilding of the Thurman Mill diversion dam into what is now officially known as the Harry Morrison Dam. Completed in 2012, the dam sits in the section of river adjacent to the popular summer recreation spot Quinn's Pond. This was the site of the 2014 Surf and Kayak Rally.

Unlike most dams built to store water and generate electricity, Morrison Dam was built not only to divert water for irrigation but also to create and shape waves that kayakers and surfers could ride. Wirelessly controlled by a laptop, pneumatic air bladders installed at the dam inflate and deflate, which in turn elevate stainless steel flashboards. This control, coupled with the water flow levels discharged from Lucky Peak Dam far upriver, determines the shape and size of the waves.

City of Boise employee Ryan Ricardo was in charge of creating two separate waves on the day of the 2014 Surf and Kayak Rally. Demonstrating the full range of the dam's abilities, Ricardo modified the waves while professional surfers and kayakers played on his creations. Through a loudspeaker, an announcer described the wave changes to the crowd gathered to watch.

The city hired Ricardo in 2013 to work as a wave technician. Young and energetic, Ricardo was a natural fit for the job of working with the kayaking and surfing crowd. According to Ricardo, multiple factors affect the wave shape. First, the waves he creates are "completely dependent" on the amount of water discharged by Lucky Peak Dam upriver. During times of high river flow, he creates two separate waves. Conversely, during times of low flows such as later in the summer, there is only sufficient water to create a single wave. Another primary factor affecting wave shaping is the dual nature of the Harry Morrison Dam. Ricardo noted that many people in the community don't understand that the

Water is diverted from the Boise River for irrigation.

primary function of the dam is to divert water for irrigation. The dam's irrigation purpose takes precedence over recreation. Ricardo must closely monitor the amount of water directed to the irrigation canal because thousands of acres of farmland depend on receiving the proper amount of water. Too much or too little water directed toward irrigation can have disastrous consequences for the farms. Consequently, during times of low flow, Ricardo has less latitude to make changes to the surfing wave.

Ricardo shows up at the river park almost every day. He attempts to alternate days between waves that are preferred by kayakers versus a wave shape preferred by surfers. Ricardo routinely posts selfie-style cell phone videos to the Boise River Park Facebook page. His videos describe the wave and any other relevant information that users need to know before heading down to the river park.

Surfing

Generally speaking, surfers prefer waves that are glassy and smooth. The wave has to be steep and fast enough to hold the surfboard in the wave. Kayakers, on the other hand, tend to like what is known as a retentive wave, which has frothier whitewater behind it. This type of wave allows kayakers to ride and perform tricks in the wave without getting pushed out. Ricardo can cater waves to individual users while sitting on the riverside with his laptop. He has developed relationships with many of the recreationists and consequently knows their individual preferences.

Christopher Peterson catching waves

A former kayaker, Ricardo has caught the surfing bug. The learning curve for river surfing is not as steep as that for ocean surfing, he said. Ocean surfing requires a lot of paddling and positioning for a mere 10-second ride. In contrast, once a river surfer learns to balance on the board, the ride on the stationary wave might end only when those surfers waiting in line grow impatient. Ricardo witnessed numerous surfers pick up the sport over the course of the summer. Some were able to quickly evolve from first-time beginners learning to merely stand on the board to proficient surfers "ripping across the face" of the wave.

Christopher Peterson was one of the surfers who benefitted from Ricardo's wave-shaping skills at the Surf and Kayak Rally. In laid-back surfer fashion, Peterson described the rally as "just another day surfing." He estimated that at least

500 spectators looked on as the surfers and kayakers turned and twisted. A highlight of the event for Peterson was meeting a contingent of German surfers who had traveled to Idaho to participate in the event. This was noteworthy because some people track the origins of river surfing back to Germany. River enthusiasts have been surfing the Eisbach River flowing through Munich for decades.

Peterson noted that river surfing in Boise is beginning to catch on as a result of the new wave-shaping dam. He estimated that there are 50 regulars down at the wave with many more in town that dabble in the sport. The river

Surfers frequent the wave-shaping feature of the Boise River Park.

park's proximity to the greenbelt as well as to the 36th Street pedestrian bridge (which connects the Live, Work, Create District, also known as the Waterfront District, in Garden City with Esther Simplot Park in Boise) attracts curious onlookers. Peterson said that it is not uncommon to have 100 people gathered on the shore watching the surfers on a warm summer evening.

To capitalize on the growing popularity of the sport, Peterson shapes and sells surfboards out of his backyard shop. To date, he has shaped about 30 boards. Surfboards intended for river waves have specific parameters that differ from ocean surfboards. First, they have a "low rocker," which means that they don't have much of a curve from tail to nose. A 20-inch width is typical with a full versus a pointy nose. Finally, the buoyancy of the board is critical. River surfboards have to be buoyant enough to support a surfer on a standing wave. This is in contrast to thinner, less buoyant ocean surfboards that are propelled forward by a powerful wave.

Peterson encountered resistance when he first began surfing the Boise River. Naysayers, to include some of his old ocean surfing friends, questioned why anyone would want to surf on a river. Bringing surfing, a sport linked with coastline, to the interior was a bit too much for some people. But, with the growing popularity of the sport, Peterson grinned, "many critics have turned into the biggest addicts."

Peterson is quick to list the advantages of river surfing in Boise. He said that although the surfing in Hawaii is tremendous, the season lasts only 4 months out of the year. One can travel to the Oregon and Washington coast to surf, but conditions there are windy, foggy, and cold. In contrast, the consistent wave at the Boise River Park can be surfed 8 months out of the year. As for weather, locals know that the sun rarely hides for long in Boise, Idaho.

New Dam Improves River Safety

The festive atmosphere of the Surf and Kayak Rally marked a sharp contrast to the tragedy that had occurred at this same site four summers earlier. On August 1, 2010, 20-year-old Cassie Conley was fatally injured at the site of the current Morrison Dam. Conley, a mother of two small children, had been tubing in this notoriously dangerous section of river. Before the construction of the Morrison Dam and its surf wave, Thurman Mill diversion dam stood in its place. The nearly 100-year-old diversion dam created a strong undertow that held Conley underwater and ultimately led to her death. A local news station reported that three other water rescues had occurred at the diversion dam in the 2 weeks before Conley's death.

The reconstruction of the Thurman Mill diversion dam, beyond its recreational and irrigation purposes, was undertaken for safety reasons. "The original premise of the Boise River Park," according to Tom Governale the Superintendent of Parks for the City of Boise, "was to make this section of the river safer." Following the death of Cassie Conley and other similar incidents at this location, the Thurman Mill diversion became the "poster-child" that helped to further rally support in the community for the rebuilding of the dam.

Kayaker throws a move.

Paul Collins echoed Superintendent Governale's account. Collins, a local physician and longtime kayaker, served as the board president of Friends of the Park. This volunteer-led organization partnered with the City of Boise in raising funds and planning for the Boise River Park. It was Friends of the Park who organized the 2014 Surf and Kayak Rally.

Collins and a few other prominent local kayakers first sat down over drinks nearly 25 years ago and hashed out the idea of building a kayak wave on the Boise River. In spring 1998, Collins and these other kayakers approached Governale about making a water feature in the river. They soon discovered that the process would be much more complicated than simply "moving some rocks around in the river." Many stakeholders, including irrigators, federal entities, and environmental regulators, would have to be consulted and their views considered.

Planners decided that the new wave-shaping feature should ideally replace one of the hazardous diversion dams located on the river. Speaking generally of diversion dams, Chief Roberts of the Boise Fire Department noted that they are extremely dangerous. During high water flows, the dams create a "horizontal whirlpool," known in his industry as a "drowning machine." Once caught in the whirlpool, people have a difficult time swimming out.

Ultimately, the Thurman Mill diversion was slated for reconstruction. Prior to its rebuild, the Thurman Mill diversion created a kayaking play wave during high water flows. Collins and other kayakers recreated at this spot, but Collins admitted it really wasn't made for "human consumption." One of the great successes and surprises for Collins has been the popularity of surfing on the shapeable wave. He said that the original planners had no idea that there would be surfing at the wave when they were working to create the park for kayakers.

The process of building the Morrison Dam, from inception to construction, was long and difficult. Raising money for the park was a challenge for Friends of the Park volunteers as their efforts coincided with the economic downturn. Believing in their vision, however, they refused to give up and just "kept asking." Collins noted that one of the great things about Boise is that "there are people that are willing to provide time, energy, and money" to projects like this, and many of these individuals take no credit. He said the community will never know about many of the people that selflessly gave to the project.

Workers install the flashboards in the WaveShaper III.

Collins also credited Superintendent Governale's "superb" leadership for making the river park happen. It was Governale that secured city funding, spearheaded the management of the permit process, and negotiated with the various stakeholders. Throughout the process, Governale worked closely with the Thurman Mill board of directors and then president Mike Matzdorf. The agreement forged between the City of Boise and the Thurman Mill irrigation district was unprecedented. Governale noted that this was "the first time in Idaho that an irrigation company entered into an agreement with a public entity to benefit public recreation." The irrigators received a new dam while Boise kayakers and surfers had their wave.

Boise River Park, Phase II

The 36th Street pedestrian bridge spans the Boise River within view of the Harry Morrison Dam. It is December 2014, and a large, bold-lettered red sign hanging on the bridge warns of DANGER and HAZARDOUS AREAS downstream. Old concrete, rebar, and jagged metal can be found in the river just downstream from the wave-shaping dam. This section of river, near the Farmer's Union diversion approximately a quarter mile downriver from the Harry Morrison Dam, has a long history of neglect and abuse. Kayakers, surfers, and other recreationists are warned by the sign to stay away from these downriver hazards as they could cause injury to people and damage to equipment.

Hazard signs displayed on the 36th Street pedestrian bridge

According to Superintendent Governale, the City of Boise will work on removing these hazards during a second phase of the Boise River Park. The plan is to build three more waves that can be used for recreation. Following the precedent set with the Harry Morrison Dam, the city will partner with Farmer's Union to ensure that their irrigation water needs continue to be met. Unlike the dynamic wave at Harry Morrison Dam, the three new waves are intended to be static structures. The uppermost drop will use a wide-crested weir with flap gates. The lower two drops will have a less forceful wave, which makes them perfect for beginner and intermediate kayakers.

When Phase II of the Boise River Park is completed, Boise will have two distinct sections of the river to recreate on: (1) the traditional tube float route from Barber Park to Ann Morrison Park, and (2) the Boise River Park. As it stands, these two sections of the river are separated by the formidable Settler's diversion dam located at Americana Bridge. This dam creates a 4-foot drop in the river that is not safe for tubing or surfing. The few tubers and rafters that float below the traditional take-out must portage around the diversion dam or they risk getting caught in a "horizontal whirlpool," as described by Chief Roberts.

Twisted metal and other dangers lurk along the Boise River.

Some people, including Superintendent Governale and Dr. Collins, envision that another partnership could be forged to replace Settler's diversion dam in the same manner that the Thurman Mill diversion dam was replaced. With this dam addressed, recreationists could float the Boise River continuously from Barber Park through the Boise River Park and beyond. Nearly the entire section of river within the city of Boise would be accessible for river sports.

River sports enthusiasts have long recreated on the cool waters of the Boise River steadily flowing through the heart of the city. Through control and management, the river evolved over time while recreation on the river persisted and grew. Tubers, rafters, kayakers, surfers, and paddleboarders have capitalized on the management of the river and have effected change to the river themselves. They look forward to this trend continuing well into the future.

TRAVIS ARMSTRONG is drawn to the backcountry and can often be found running, mountain biking, or motorcycling in Idaho's mountains and deserts. Travis writes about the unique ways that Idahoans explore and experience their beautiful state.

5 | History along the Greenbelt

Relics and storied places connect Boise to frontier past.

by Doug Copsey, with Todd Shallat

The Boise educates and irrigates. Suspended between engineering and nature—a floodway, a ribbon of settlement, a fishery, and a sewer for dangerous toxins—the river is also a cultural landmark. Its history connects the city to an ancient landscape. A historical appreciation of those gentle waters flowing can nourish our urban souls.

Stone-age nomads left their mark on the river's valley in petroglyphs pecked into blackened boulders torn from the cliffs during ancient floods. Their descendants who settled along the river became known as Snakes for the snake figures on sticks once used to mark territory. Nineteenth-century fur traders mostly referred to them by their language, calling them Shoshone and Paiutes. Over time, the Boise Valley became a regional free-trade for travels from dozens of tribes. By 1810, mounted Paiutes called Bannock fished in the Boise River en route from Oregon to Yellowstone buffalo hunts. Sahaptini, or Nez Perce as the French traders called them, rode down from the North.

French, British, and American trappers rushed the Snake River basin for furs soon after Lewis and Clark. Scottish-Canadian Donald MacKenzie reached the Boise in 1811. Weeks later a greenhorn merchant named Wilson Price Hunt reported well-dressed Shoshone near the future town of Parma. Ragged and near starvation, Hunt traded for dogs and horsemeat. Hunt's map called the river "Wood" for its cottonwoods and willows. "Wood" became *Boisse*, *Borssie*, or *Boisey* in French translations. An 1812 sketch map of southern Idaho named the river for American trapper John Reed. Another 20 years would pass before essayist Washington Irving created the legend that Captain Bonneville and his brigade of French trappers named the valley when they crested the foothills and shouted, "les bois, les bois," meaning "the trees, the trees," on seeing it for the first time.

Natives, highly mobile, migrated in and out the Boise, stopping near the future city for trade and trout. British trappers built small flood-prone trading posts—one near future Middleton, another on marshland near Parma where the Boise entered the Snake. From 1842 to 1862, during the era of the Oregon Trail, native spear-fishers sustained the wagon migration. Perhaps 300,000 whites with massive herds of cattle and

oxen passed through the Boise Valley. In 1849, when Idaho was part of the Oregon Territory newly annexed from Britain, U.S. troops surveyed the river. Five years later, near Middleton, a Shoshone attack on the Alexander Ward wagon train may have been British inspired.

Gold and the Civil War brought settlers to the Boise River. In 1862, on a mountain tributary of the Boise River, a gold strike ignited the boom. Perhaps 20,000 miners rushed to Boise Mountain in April of the following year. On April 4, 1863, President Abraham Lincoln signed the congressional act that created Idaho Territory. To police the new territory, and guard the gold, Major Pinkney Lugenbeel led a union

President Lincoln carved Idaho from the Oregon Territory during the Boise Basin gold rush of 1863.

regiment, heavily armed, to a height on land overlooking the mule trail to the Boise gold rush. United States Fort Boise founded the namesake city that grew to become the largest on the Oregon Trail.

More than a hundred years later, the Ada County Centennial Committee's "History along the Greenbelt" program produced markers along the trail identifying historical sites, and Chairman Jim Witherell undertook the task of researching and writing a reference book that could be used as a field guide for teachers. The stories he discovered are pictures of a culture still nourished by this shining ribbon as it carves its way through our lives today.

Mining and Irrigation

To begin at the beginning, mount your bicycle at Discovery State Park, just below Lucky Peak Dam. It was here that Arthur Foote built a house for his genteel wife, Mary Hallock Foote, who traveled to Kuna by stagecoach and arrived in Boise City in 1884. She was a proper Victorian from New York, with hoops and petticoats, but she quickly grew to love the rugged western country in which she found herself. Already a well-known author and illustrator in the East, her celebrity grew through the stories she told of the rough, picturesque life in the early mining boomtowns for publications such as *Century Magazine*.

Arthur De Wint Foote
1849-1933

Arthur had come here to implement the Idaho Mining and Irrigation Company's ambitious plan to build a 75-mile canal and 5,000 miles of laterals that would use Boise River water to irrigate some 500,000 acres of farmland. A financial panic in 1884 ruined some investors, others backed out, and Foote began surveying for a less ambitious irrigation network. At last, in 1890, the twice bankrupted canal project ran water from the Boise River to Nampa. But it quickly became apparent that a dam and reservoir were needed to increase the flow.

By 1905, after Congress established the U.S. Reclamation Service, the government town of Diversion Dam had an estimated population of 250. Mostly a tent city, it was dismantled when the dam was commissioned in 1909, only to be resurrected after the droughts of 1909–1910 proved the reservoir inadequate, and a larger site, dubbed Arrowrock, was selected farther upriver. The only remnant is a caretaker's house along the greenbelt just below the dam.

A private road leading to Barber Dam just off the bike path is all that remains of Silk Stocking Row, the first street in the town of Barber. In 1906, the Barber Lumber Company ran a two-band sawmill and a wooden plank dam, and the last milltown built in Idaho had 650 residents over 18 square blocks with steam-heated homes, a hotel, a community hall, its own municipal water system, a school system, and, in 1915, a sewer system. It was also rumored to be the moonshine capital of the valley.

Heading east for the next 2 miles, the bike path runs over an old railroad bed, originally the Intermountain Railway, incorporated to move timber from Grimes and Mores Creeks to the Barber mill. In 1910, the U.S. Reclamation Service built the Boise & Arrowrock Railroad, not only to haul timber from the mountains but to haul the hordes of tourists flocking to see the spectacle of Arrowrock Dam, the tallest in the world until Hoover Dam was built in the 1930s. A round-trip ticket cost

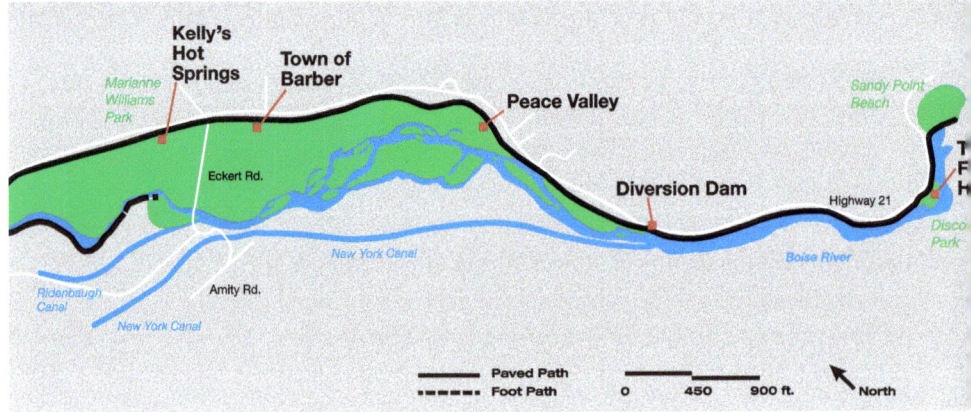

$2.00, an average day's wage at the time. The Inaugural Special on October 4, 1915, carried 2,000 people in a single trip to witness the commissioning of the dam. During this time, four railroads came together at Eckert Road, and between 1912 and 1915, nearly 90,000 passengers changed trains.

About a quarter mile west, the largest of three hot springs in the valley poured out the mouth of the small canyon below today's Warm Springs Mesa. In 1870, mineral baths were considered a cure-all, and J.L. Stephens, a local physician, claimed them for a therapeutic spa. Four years later, a mud bath, steam plunge, dance hall, and café were added and things went swimmingly for another 15 years.

That's when *Idaho Statesman* editor Milton Kelly bought the springs, added a hotel, remodeled all the facilities, and held a grand opening for Kelly's Hot Springs to draw attention from the newly opened Natatorium, a short distance downstream. Besides being too far out of town, spa prices were more than most Boiseans could afford, so Kelly turned the resort into a private club and began serving liquor. Kelly's Warm Springs resort, it was alleged, became a member-only brothel. When the resort burned down the second time in 1911 – temperance groups were suspected of arson both times – the owners finally called it quits.

The Natatorium, built 1892, was one of the largest indoor spas in the United States, rising six stories and covering 150,000 square feet. Its 400-foot well produced a stable flow of 800,000 cubic feet per day at a constant 112 degrees. There were 50 dressing rooms, parlors, billiard rooms, cafés on three levels, and a formal dining room. A cover slid over the 65 × 125 foot pool so it could serve as a dance floor and roller skating rink. By this time, entrepreneurs had developed the river's floodplain by investing in electric streetcars. The "Nat" soon became a permanent terminus for the Boise Rapid Transit, bringing bathers from all over the city down the bumpy, dirt road called Warm Springs Avenue to Boise's most luxurious entertainment spot.

The Natatorium on Warm Springs Avenue, built in 1892

The most successful of these entrepreneurs was a real estate investor from Kansas City named Walter E. Pierce, who had gotten himself elected Mayor of Boise. When he announced plans to build a boating park on the river west of Collister Street, competitors at the Nat beat him to the punch, naming their private park after Chicago's famous White City fairgrounds. Boise's White City opened in the summer of 1907 with a roller coaster, a miniature railway, carousel, photography studio, an outdoor dance pavilion that also doubled as a roller rink, and a boating pond that was later replaced with a penny arcade and concession stands.

After absorbing 40 years' worth of mineral steam, the wooden structure around the pool had rotted, and a 1934 windstorm collapsed part of the roof. The building was torn down, but the pool, being the only one in town, was purchased by the city and still operates. White City survived until WWII, when the aging wooden roller coaster was condemned. The property was purchased by the Boise School District, and Adams Elementary School stands there today.

Amusing the Masses

A short ride farther downriver brings you to Municipal Park, originally purchased in 1910 by the Boise School District to build a sports stadium that never materialized. In 1918 the Boise Commercial Club leased it as a campground for the steady stream of "auto tramps" seeking work on Idaho farms. There was a communal kitchen with 14 hotplates, a washing machine, a playground, and two cement slabs for washing cars. The only charge was a 25 cent per car donation to pay for electricity. The first seasons saw more than 6,000 carloads of campers.

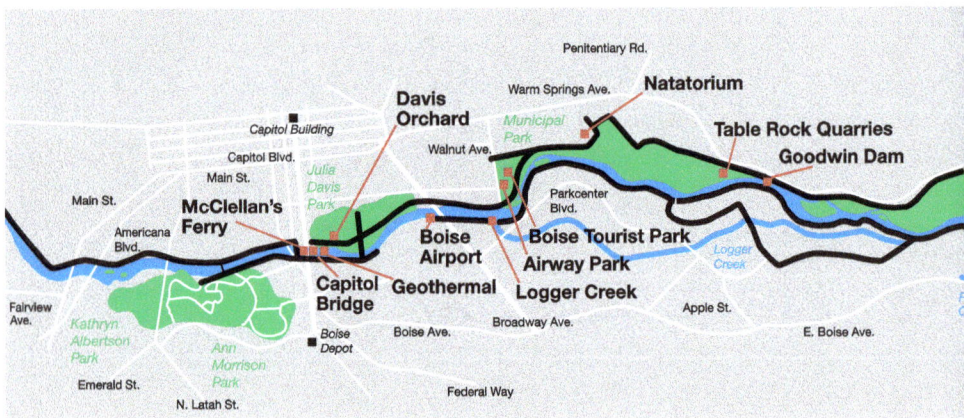

After 1918, when Idaho paved the Lincoln Highway, motor tourists flooded Municipal Park. Annually, the park received an estimated 20,000 carloads. Many car-campers stayed more than a week, prompting the city to add a bathhouse. Vagrancy forced the city to close the park to camping in 1938.

Baseball took center stage at the close of the Great Depression. In 1939, where the Idaho Fish and Game Department now stands at Park and Walnut, Airway Park began as a crude stadium with a couple of admission boxes. It became home to a fully franchised, Class C, professional Pioneer League team called the Boise Pilots. Spokane sports mogul Haydn Walker bought a controlling interest that year and built a new, 3,000-seat stadium. It was increased to 5,000 seats after WWII, and when the Pittsburgh Pirates came to town for an exhibition game in 1958, more than 7,000 fans crammed inside to watch their team get trounced 17-6. By that time the Pilots had become the Braves, an affiliate of the Milwaukee Braves, and attendance continued to increase, topping 36,000 in 1957. The league finally folded in 1963 and a year later, Fish and Game picked up the property.

As the greenbelt crosses under Broadway Avenue, Albertson's Stadium, home of the Boise State Broncos, looms along the south bank of the river, but in 1926 this wedge of bottomland was a city dump. That same year the federal government created a new airmail route from Elko to Pasco via Boise. The only airport at the time was a private strip on the first bench, but it was unsuitable in wet weather and too far from the city.

The City Council decided to use the Broadway land and purchase an adjoining 30 acres known as the Booth tract, but that left them with no money to build the airport. The Chamber of Commerce agreed to buy the needed materials, and the American Legion volunteered the labor for buildings and runway construction. Mail service was inaugurated on April 6, 1926. When Congress passed airline passenger subsidies in 1930, United Airlines bought the mail operation and put Boise on a route that included Salt Lake City, Portland, and Seattle. Even though the airline built a new, 145 × 85 foot brick and glass terminal building, Boise outgrew Booth Field virtually overnight, and in 1936 the City Council relocated the airport to its present site.

First airmail flight from Boise, April 6, 1926, with Governor H.C. Baldridge and Boise Mayor Walter F. Hansen

Long before Boise entered the air age, Thomas Jefferson Davis filed one of the first homestead claims in Idaho Territory on the opposite side of the river. In 1863, his initial 320-acre claim included sections of what is now downtown Boise and the bottomland along the north bank of the river between

Broadway and 8th Street, where he planted 7,000 fruit trees, creating the Davis Orchard. In 1871 he married Julia McCrum, and on her death in 1907, he donated 40 acres of the orchard to the city as a public park in her memory.

The city spent years reclaiming flood lands along the north side of the river, and by 1915 Julia Davis Park had become a popular destination. But across the river, near the future site of the Morrison Center, abandoned car bodies and other refuse from that extensive reclamation project had become an illegal dump. A renovation program in 1926 put a concrete pillar and iron gate at the 8th Street entrance, shortened the road to exit onto Myrtle Street, and added the bandshell. Over the years the Davis Estate donated more land, and so did Morrison-Knudsen Company, which owned the pond at the east end, and the park grew to its present size, except for a few acres lost when Capitol Boulevard came through in 1931.

John McClellan's ferry at the foot of 7th Street, Boise, about 1864

When Boise was first settled, the lands now occupied by Boise State University (BSU) and Ann Morrison Park were shifting flood-prone islands in the 600-foot meandering channel. In the summer of 1863, William Thompson, a physician, and freighter John McClellan both claimed land on 8th Street for the city's first wagon ferry. Expensive and, said a traveler, "a miserable one-horse affair," the ferry charged 25 cents per person and another 75 cents for a horse. Loaded pack animals were 25 cents each; loose animals, 12 cents; sheep or hogs, 5 cents; and a wagon with team, a whopping $2.25. In 1867, the partners opened a toll bridge and doubled the prices. As Boise grew, more and more citizens complained about having to pay to cross the river. In 1911 the city and the Oregon Short Line built a rail and pedestrian bridge.

Around 1880, when displaced Chinese railroad and mine laborers began to turn to market gardens for their income, Tom Davis leased them land where BSU now stands. It was of little value, being across the river and accessible only by toll bridge or boat, and frequent flooding often destroyed crops. So Davis offered 800 acres of pastureland about a mile downriver that had been an army hay field during the early days of Fort Boise, and by 1890 upward of 1,000 immigrants were working an area along the south bank of the river known as the New Chinese Gardens.

Chinese gardener stands by his Model T in the 1920s

The backyard Victory Garden that emerged during WWI ruined the demand for vegetable markets. The Chinese protested in 1918, saying their livelihood was endangered, but by that time non-Chinese produce was flooding the market, brought in by truck from outlying areas. Residential development moved in, and by 1937 the newspaper speculated there were only two or three gardeners left. The final blow came in 1949, when a state law introduced slot-machine gambling. Boise businessmen incorporated the area as Garden City and opened several casinos. Until the law was repealed in 1953, the area was known as Little Reno.

Old Soldiers

After the Civil War ended, a fraternal organization known as the Grand Army of the Republic managed to secure a small pension for veterans and invented the concept of Soldiers Homes to care for aged, destitute, or disabled veterans. Idaho Territory had no militia during the Civil War, but when it became a state and gained ownership of federal endowment lands, the Grand Army of the Republic immediately began

The Idaho Soldiers Home on the future site of Veteran's Park

a campaign for an Idaho Soldiers Home. Three Boise businessmen anonymously donated 40 acres of land along the north bank of the river on Valley Road, now State Street, and raised almost $5,000 from the public for construction.

The cornerstone was laid on May 23, 1894, and 10 veterans were admitted as soon as the first two of three stories were completed. After WWI, the home had 120 residents, a barracks was added, and the dispensary was replaced by a small hospital. It served veterans of six wars for 71 years, but after WWII the State began to shift responsibility for the home to the Veterans Administration, and a public move began to close the building as a relic. Today the Boise River Greenbelt winds past the original 38-acre campus in the midst of a 200-acre Veterans Park.

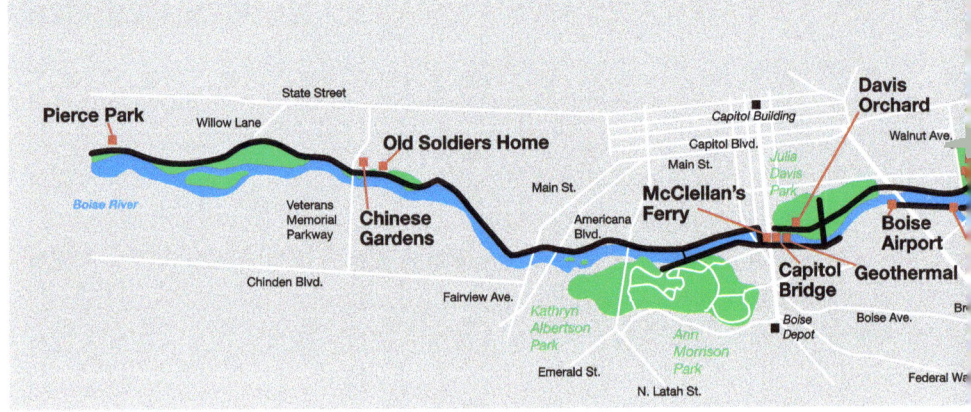

West of the park, the river flows past the Plantation Golf Course. Not dissuaded when his rivals built White City at the Natatorium, W.E. Pierce opened his own amusement park here on Labor Day 1907. Second only to White City, it had a baseball field, a bandstand, refreshment stand, tennis courts, and croquet plots. Two years later an artificial lake 250 feet wide and 3 feet deep was dredged out for rowboats, and in 1912, a dance pavilion rounded out the facilities. Like its rival on the east side of town, a Boise & Interurban Railway station was close by.

Ironically, through a series of mergers, Pierce lost control of the park, only to purchase the Natatorium and White City a few years later and compete with his namesake. By 1928 the park was obsolete and the property was purchased by the Plantation Company, which kept the dance pavilion and, in 1932, built a golf course.

The river below its namesake city drains a board-flat patchwork of farmland, becoming a nutrient-rich dark green to its confluence with the Snake. More than 20 major canals tap the river for agriculture. Leveed for farms and subdivisions, the river is no longer the braided stream made famous by Washington Irving. Culturally, nevertheless, in its paths and historical markers, memories of that river remain.

Boise River irrigation at Joplin Farm, Nampa

DOUG COPSEY is a writer, director, producer, and current president of the Idaho Writers Guild. He has written screenplays, essays, and magazine articles, as well as a history of the Idaho Shakespeare Festival (*With Our Good Will – 30 Years of Shakespeare in Idaho*), which he founded. He is currently at work on his second novel.

TODD SHALLAT, Ph.D. (Carnegie Mellon University), directs the Center for Idaho History and Politics at Boise State University. He specializes in the history of science, technology, and the environment.

6 | The Waterfront District

Garden City bridges the river via parks and urban renewal.

by Sheila Spangler

In Garden City, near East 36th and North Adams Streets, the bright future of a new kind of urban living emerges from a blighted meatpacking site. Developers call it the Waterfront District. Its riverside townhouses face a public beach and the new whitewater park. A footbridge crosses to Esther Simplot Park and Boise's newest urban renewal district, with plans for bike paths, streetcars, and mixed-used shopping nodes.

Conceived in 2007, the waterfront bridged many constituencies. Kayakers wanted boulders in the river to create an urban whitewater experience. Boise City Council wanted high-density infill. The Ada County Highway District wanted a 30th Street traffic connection from State Street to the I-184 Connector. A real estate developer dreamed of a riverfront subdivision. In 2015, as public funding joins private investment, people who treasure the river are reclaiming an industrial stretch of the Boise floodplain and charting a more profitable path.

The River and Its Players

The story begins with a group of kayakers—Jo Cassin, Stan Kolby, and Paul Collins—who managed to convince a city government to build a whitewater park in the urban Boise River. According to Cassin, co-owner of Idaho River Sports, beginning in the late 1980s several individuals with varying interests about water usage in the Boise River got together. "This was just a group of Boise River users with different backgrounds and different ideas and plans who came together to make it work for everyone." This group was formed at the prompting of Pete Zimowsky, long-time outdoors reporter for the *Idaho Statesman*, and Paul Collins, a local physician and whitewater enthusiast. The Boise River 2000 Group consisted of recreationists, environmentalists, irrigators, state agencies, state representatives, and those involved in noxious weed eradication and flood control. "Basically, we would float certain sections of the Boise River in canoes or rafts. Each group would talk about what their needs were," said Cassin. She learned about different issues affecting the various users.

People concerned about flood control wanted to maintain as little water as possible in Lucky Peak Reservoir in case of a quick snowmelt or heavy rain. Irrigators wanted to maintain as much water as possible for agricultural production. Environmentalists and Idaho Fish and Game officials worried about the volume and speed of the river flow and how it negatively impacted the vegetation and fish.

After several seasons of performing this adjunct unofficial impact study, Collins, Cassin, and Kolby approached the City of Boise requesting that some boulders be placed in the river to create a whitewater experience. This request launched the intent to build a river park. "Never underestimate the power of a few," Tom Governale, Boise's superintendent of parks said.

Industries, such as lumberyards, dumped their waste into the Boise River.

The Barber Lumber company was located in South Boise near the present-day Marianne Williams Park.

Until the 1960s, the few who valued the section of the river west of downtown Boise were the owners of industrial processing plants. Most used it as junkyard and sewer for waste from slaughterhouses or to obtain water for concrete plants. In part due to former Boise City Council member Bill Onweiler's promotion of the idea for a greenbelt, City of Boise officials gained a new perspective about how the river figured prominently in the city's future. In *When the River Rises: Flood Control on the Boise River 1943-1985*, Susan M. Stacy wrote, "In the early 1960s Boise officials determined it was time ... to do some general comprehensive land use planning." The city hired Harold E. Atkinson, a planning consultant from California. In his report, he suggested that the city "acquire land along the Boise River so as to create a continuous greenbelt of public lands stretching along the river throughout the entire length of the community." Atkinson's report emphasized that with Boise as the state capital, "it has more than the usual need and opportunity for parks and green areas" and that "physical enhancement is a particularly worthwhile community goal." Atkinson's report catalyzed the city's acquisition of the land along the river through purchases and easements to create the Boise River Greenbelt.

Atkinson's recommendation and Onweiler's promotion of a river greenbelt owe their genesis to the construction of Lucky Peak Dam in 1955. The main concerns for the residents of the Treasure Valley in the 1950s regarding the Boise River centered on the timing and volume of water release from the dam to maintain sufficient resources for irrigators and to reduce the threat of flooding. Awareness of the river and its potential additional urban amenities changed in the 1960s as a result of Atkinson's report, but little happened during the next 25 years. Gravel pit operators continued mining from riverside quarries, farmers pastured their livestock along the river banks, and lumberyards and food processors dumped their effluent into the passing stream. In fact, parents warned their children to stay out of the river because it was so polluted. Although the City of Boise stopped pouring its raw sewage into the river in 1950, the treatment plants dumped more and more detergent into the water, and, according to Stacy's research, the food processors continued to deposit "grease, potato peelings, beet pulp, blood and manure" into the river. Despite the industrial sludge, kids floated the river on inner tubes during the sweltering southern Idaho summers, but they stayed far upstream from the "slime beds" west of downtown.

A pollution warning is posted on the Boise River.

Efforts to clean up the river became critically important after the passage of the Clean Water Act in 1972. This act provided the means for the U.S. Army Corps of Engineers to "provide technical assistance to local communities as they planned alternatives to dumping untreated wastes in rivers." Federal and local agencies worked together to clean up the river. These joint efforts led to the construction of a wastewater treatment plant in Boise and other measures to reduce pollution caused by industrial users. In addition, the general public became enthusiastic supporters of creating a greenbelt designed for those who wanted to walk, bike, fish, tube, or raft the Boise River. Thus began the transformation of the Boise River from industrial tool to economic and recreational amenity.

Kayakers wait for their turn to ride the wave.

Whitewater Bonanza

Launched in 2012, the Boise River Park serves as an economic development tool in the Treasure Valley. Although no formal report has been made on the potential economic impact of the Boise River Park, other similar projects in western U.S. communities forecast a positive economic outcome. Steamboat Springs Whitewater Park in Colorado estimated its total potential economic benefit at $7.2 million per year. (According to the 2010 census report, the population of Steamboat Springs was 12,088 people. In comparison, Boise was home to 210,000 residents in 2010.) The Truckee River Recreation Plan, a whitewater park in Reno-Sparks, Nevada, was estimated to bring in $1.9 million in its first year. Similarly, the Clear Creek Whitewater Park in Golden, Colorado, projected the recreational and beneficial use values between $1.36 million and $2.03 million annually.

Local Boise businessman Clay Carley champions waterfront development. Carley, son of the founder of Old Boise historical district and owner of the Owyhee Plaza, sees river recreation as a way for a city in isolation to market its amenities. "We are isolated, yet we want to grow up," Carley said from his office on Main Street. Carley explained that it is difficult to translate quality-of-life features into financial reasons for companies to relocate their workforces here. "We were once in the top 10 budding high-tech communities— when Micron and HP [Hewlett-Packard] were moving ahead. We didn't recognize the power of that and take advantage of it." He believes that the community missed an early opportunity to encourage and promote computer science degrees and to get funding to bring in more high-tech businesses to create what he called a "critical mass."

Yet Carley saw the recently constructed river park as a way to attract and retain new businesses. "It is a unique amenity that sets us apart. ... We have to build attraction on lifestyle. It's slow and painful, but it does work." Carley spoke from experience as one of several fundraisers for Friends of the Parks, a group of volunteers formed primarily to raise money to construct the Boise River Park. Carley had raised funds for other causes, but this one was the most challenging because of its single-purpose use and small niche. Among the many causes competing for donation dollars, "boating is a weird thing to raise money for," Carley admitted. "Most people that are passionate about it have no money." His team's fundraising efforts garnered close to $1 million for phase I of the Boise River Park.

In addition to the money raised by Carley and Friends of the Parks, three local foundations contributed significant amounts to the renewal of the west end of Boise and to the creation of two of Boise's newest parks, the Boise River Park and Esther Simplot Park. J.R. Simplot, Joe Albertson, and Harry Morrison created what became multimillion-dollar companies in Boise at roughly the same time; these companies are Simplot Company, a producer of agriculture-related products; Albertsons, a national grocery store chain;

and Morrison-Knudsen, an international engineering and construction contractor (purchased by Washington Group International in 1996 and merged into URS Corporation in 2007). All three businessmen formed nonprofit foundations to funnel a good portion of their wealth into local causes. (Years later, J.R. Simplot's grandson, J.D. Simplot, would play a role in waterfront renewal by arranging the financing for the construction of the Waterfront subdivision in Garden City.)

Besides the philanthropy of wealthy individuals, the willing participation of city government also played a large role in the redevelopment of the Waterfront District. According to Elaine Clegg, a Boise City Council member, the city invested approximately $2 million in a hydrology study and floodway structure that made Esther Simplot Park possible. This study also provided the information necessary to protect Garden City in the event of a flood. Garden City changed its comprehensive plan, altered its zoning ordinance, and made some needed infrastructure changes. "These kinds of efforts rarely happen because one player says 'I am going to do it,'" Clegg asserted. "They happen because multiple players, even some with competing visions, figure out a way to work together so everyone's vision can work."

Clegg emphasized that the City of Boise, specifically the Public Works and Parks Department and Planning and Development services, helped craft a vision for the entire area surrounding the Esther Simplot Park. This area was recorded as the West End plat in 1903. By 1906, a lumber mill was constructed on the east side of the river occupying the same geographic area as the new Esther Simplot Park, scheduled to open in spring 2016. Slaughterhouses, petroleum tank farms, gravel pits, and car lots made up some of the commercial business activity in this area during the 1920s. In 1992, the Interstate 184 Connector provided a bypass for automobile traffic, and the area experienced an economic decline. The construction of Whitewater Boulevard by the Ada County Highway District in 2012 provided a thoroughfare from State Street to Fairview Avenue to the I-184 Connector. According to Clegg, getting a new arterial corridor in a mature neighborhood is "pretty unusual." In 2013, the neighborhood was rechristened with its original name, the West End.

Clegg visualized the revitalization of the West End neighborhood long before she joined the Boise City Council. "We had all this land so near downtown being ignored and underutilized and yet it had all these assets—the river, the greenbelt, proximity to downtown, and a historic neighborhood," Clegg recalled. She made it clear that without the support of fellow City Council members, the Boise Parks and Recreation Department, Ada County Highway District, and the West End Neighborhood Association, the changes would not have occurred.

A New Vision for Garden City

While the City of Boise planned the Boise River Park, the Esther Simplot Park, and the West End neighborhood, the unkempt property directly across the river in Garden City sat vacant. Looking through a bramble of blackberry bushes and blocked by a cattle gate, real estate developer Jim Neill noticed the bare 17.5-acre riverfront property at the end of 36th Street in Garden City in 2004. He quickly negotiated with the sellers to acquire the property. His ability to finance the purchase was uncertain, but he had faith it would work out.

Riverside trailer, Garden City, 2014

Although no one person was responsible for Garden City's recent transformation, Jim Neill was acknowledged as a catalyst for change by those who worked with him. Neill invested his entire life savings and devoted 10 years of his life to the Waterfront District project on the Boise River in Garden City. Unable to afford to live in the subdivision he created, he lived a couple of blocks away in a place he described as a teardown. Although just a short walk from the new Waterfront District development, it was a far cry from his former residence. "I needed a roof over my head and wanted to finish what I had started," explained Neill. "It was 80% unemployment among my friends, not 8%."

Dave Green of Garden City lives with his son in a park of mobile homes slated for gentrification.

In 2004, Neill visited mixed-media artist Surel Mitchell, who lived on the corner of 33rd and Carr Streets in Garden City. Mitchell's enthusiasm about the area and the changing culture, particularly in the artistic community, intrigued Neill. After Mitchell's death in 2011, Garden City renamed the area encompassing the properties from the Boise River to the Bench and from 37th Street to the Riverside Hotel as the "Surel Mitchell Live, Work, Create District" to honor Mitchell for her instrumental efforts to create a new vision for the area. In 2012, Surel's Place was incorporated as a nonprofit artist-in-residency program using Mitchell's former home as a temporary residence-studio. According to the organization's website, the nonprofit assists struggling artists by providing free rent, utilities, and a modest stipend for a specified period.

Garden City's Waterfront District is a successful urban renewal project begun by developer Jim Neill a decade ago on land that once supported a slaughterhouse.

Near Mitchell's home and originally the site of a meatpacking plant, the property acquired by Neill was the culmination of knowing the right people at the right time and having a unique perspective on the future. The concept for the project began in 2004. According to Neill, "everyone almost had the idea, but no one knew exactly what the end result would look like." Neill credits Sherry McKibben, principal with McKibben and Cooper Architects, with understanding his vision by putting his idea on paper and making sense of it. She encouraged Neill to make the area look and feel safe.

Neill and his four partners—experienced real estate investors and builders, Gene Harding, J.D. Simplot, Peter

Harris, and David Elcox—acquired the property in spring 2005. Harris, an experienced contractor with knowledge of road construction and subdivision utility installation, commenced with the necessary work.

By December 2006, the cost of the project was approaching $6 million and all funds had been spent. Before sales of subdivision lots could begin, final plat approval was needed. This took a year and a half of public hearings, required approvals, and administrative oversight by various governmental agencies.

Neill served on the steering committee in 2006, when Garden City implemented a comprehensive plan. City code hadn't been updated for almost 20 years. Neill's involvement provided the impetus for change, according to Jenah Thornborrow, economic development officer with Garden City. "Jim definitely had a vision and while there were a number of players involved, he helped push through the comprehensive plan," she said. The property required rezoning. The old code had created a Wild West mentality without much concern for development. As a result, residential property abutted industrial lots. Garden City functioned as the literal dumping ground for businesses that the City of Boise did not want. Thornborrow indicated that changing the city code took a lot of coordination and compromise to make things work.

In yet another feat of collaboration and cooperation, Garden City and Boise constructed a footbridge across the Boise River in 2011. The bridge provided access for foot and bike traffic from 36th Street on the south side of the river in Garden City to Quinn's Pond on Pleasanton Street on the north side of the river in Boise. Garden City mayor John Evans and David Bieter, mayor of Boise, deserve credit for this unprecedented collaboration. This was a significant accomplishment and a historic occasion. As recently as 1977, former Boise mayor Dick Eardley had no kind words for Garden City or its residents. According to J.M. Neil's article, Eardley said, "A significant number of undesirables live in and operate out of Garden City. We do not want that area to expand." By 2011, a new attitude prevailed.

36th Street pedestrian bridge

Mayors Evans and Bieter and their respective staffs worked together to find a solution to create a new river experience for the community and to benefit both municipalities. The footbridge built across the river linked Boise and Garden City physically and economically. The 12-foot-wide concrete and steel beam footbridge cost $750,000. Most of the funding ($550,000) came from an American Recovery Reinvestment Act federal stimulus grant. The City of Boise covered the remaining $250,000.

The footbridge provided a physical as well as psychological connection between the two cities. Not only did it allow runners, walkers, and bike riders to cross the river, but it provided a safe route for Garden City students to attend Whittier Elementary and Anser Charter schools on the Boise side. This access enhanced the feeling of community and added to the area's livability. The bridge played a critical role in the urban renewal efforts on both sides of the river—connecting Boise's West End and Garden City's Live, Work, Create neighborhoods. The bridge was a metaphor for the future of economic development—connect, collaborate, and create. Both mayors touted the 36th Street footbridge as a "great example of neighboring cities working together to leverage resources to the benefit of the entire community."

More bridge-building occurred when Mayors Evans and Bieter negotiated to adjust the boundary lines for property on both sides of the river. Originally, Garden City's annexation encompassed the Thurman Mill diversion dam at the site of the new hydraulic whitewater wave shaper. The two city governments agreed to swap jurisdiction for the water park to the City of Boise while Garden City obtained tax revenue from Joe's Crab Shack, a Boise restaurant located upstream on the river. This made sense because the City of Boise possessed the infrastructure to manage parks and provide emergency medical, police, and fire protection. Mayor Evans believed both municipalities benefited economically because of the switch. "We all like to eat the golden egg," he said. "So we need to take care of the goose that lays it."

Farmers and the Simplot Foundation

The J.R. Simplot Foundation made it possible for City of Boise to acquire the abandoned 55 acres of land along the Boise River where the former Consolidated Concrete plant stood. This property, now the site of Esther Simplot Park, is located directly across the river from Garden City's Waterfront District housing development. The circumstances that led to the J.R. Simplot Foundation's donation took a meandering path much like the Boise River before it was channelized more than 40 years ago.

In the mid-1990s, the J.R. Simplot Foundation sold Idaho Ice World, a local ice skating rink, to the City of Boise for $1 million. At the time, the property had a value of approximately $12 million. At roughly the same time, the City of Boise negotiated a $3 million offer to acquire the 55-acre Consolidated Concrete plant property. With approximately $2 million available in its coffers, the city needed funds to complete the purchase. The J.R. Simplot Foundation returned the $1 million it had received from the City of Boise for the purchase of the Idaho Ice World property with one caveat: the 55 acres must be turned into a park named after J.R. Simplot's wife, Esther. Thus, the new park added another gem to Boise's Ribbon of Jewels, the convocation of riverside parks named after Boise patrons and wives of successful local businessmen. In addition, the J.R. Simplot Foundation committed up to $10 million for development of the Esther Simplot Park.

J.R. Simplot, 1909-2008

According to Amy Stahl, community relations manager for the Boise Parks and Recreation Department, "One of the special things about Boise is that donors have a voice in the future development and improvements that occur in the park." Scott Simplot, son of deceased industrial magnate J.R. Simplot, as vice president and director of the J.R. Simplot Foundation was instrumental in developing the park layout. Other board members include J.R. Simplot's daughter Gay Simplot, former wife of three-time Idaho governor Butch Otter; son Don Simplot; and grandchildren Debbie McDonald and Ted Simplot. The foundation board made the decision to donate funds for the park and hired a world-class design firm to create the concept. "I can't help but use superlatives," Stahl gushed, "because it will be an extraordinary conversion of an industrial property into this recreational wonderland with swimming, boating, family space, picnicking areas—all providing this interface with water." The park is scheduled to open in spring 2016.

Concurrently, the City of Boise constructed a new $1 million diversion dam with wave shapers on the river. Although the actual dam cost $1 million, superintendant of parks Governale said, other parts of the project required to support the dam pushed the price tag higher. The newly rebuilt Thurman Mill diversion dam, officially named the Harry Morrison Dam, commemorates the founder of one of the world's most successful dam-building companies, Morrison-Knudsen. According to Governale, a group of Morrison-Knudsen retirees raised $50,000 to name the dam in honor of Morrison. For the overall construction of the Boise River Park, the Harry W. Morrison Foundation contributed $200,000 in matching grants over 3 years, and the Joe and Kathryn Albertson Foundation donated $1.4 million. The overall total cost of phase I of the Boise River Park was approximately $3.6 million.

After the rebuilding of Thurman Mill diversion dam, Farmers Union inked an agreement to work with the City of Boise on the development of phase II of the Boise River Park. According to the Friends of the Park Boise River Park website, the City of Boise will spend $830,000 to replace a culvert and headgate and cover the ditch in preparation for the construction of Esther Simplot Park. The J.R. Simplot Foundation committed to construct Esther Simplot Park at a cost of approximately $10 million. Phase II of the river park will require another $2 to $3 million in private donations to augment funding from the City of Boise. The city estimated the total budget for the Boise River Park phase II at $7 million. Work on phase II of the Boise River Park began in early 2015.

The mission of an irrigation district is to protect the water rights of agricultural production users. It was unprecedented for one, let alone two, irrigation districts to willingly work with a governmental entity to allow the use of diversion dams for recreational purposes. This cooperation was essential to making the water park a reality.

Building Community

Because of the economic downturn in 2008, the Waterfront District subdivision project languished until late 2013, when lots began to sell again and building recommenced. In 2015, a mix of single-family homes, townhouses, and live-work spaces in Tuscan, modern, and other, eclectic styles lined new streets with names like Willow Bar Way and Water Pocket Lane, evocative of the newly constructed river park just a stone's throw away. "There's nothing else like it in Idaho," said Jenna King, Waterfront District resident and realtor at Keller Williams Realty Boise. From her third-floor balcony at dusk, she gazed at the lavender foothills and the emerging lights downtown Boise. Below her, neighbors with dogs socialized on a patch of grass near the site of a future clubhouse and pool. "It's 'yappy hour,'" King smiled. It took a while, but "there's a real sense of community here," she said.

That community will soon include more affordable housing. A half-block away, on 36th Street, "36 Oak" is a subdivision containing 24 small lots on which single-family homes will be built. Construction was scheduled to begin in May 2015. According to Joe Swenson, CEO of the nonprofit

Orange lines mark Boise's 30th Street "West End" urban renewal district, now linked to Garden City by footbridge.

Neighborhood Housing Services, this is one of several projects designed to bring affordable housing to the gentrified Live, Work, Create District in Garden City. Doing business as Neighborhood Homes, Neighborhood Housing Services completed and sold five homes in the range of $140,000 on East Adams Court, and it has plans for two additional pocket neighborhoods with smaller cottages on smaller lots designed to create close-knit communities with cost-efficient homes.

Whereas the neighborhood can be accessed by foot or bike or kayak from the greenbelt, drive-in access to the area is from East 36th Street off of Chinden Blvd. In 2014, Ada County Highway District added street lighting, expanded parking, installed decorative pavement, built berms, planted trees, and put in sidewalks along 36th Street. The project cost approximately $550,000.

Years from now when the Waterfront District becomes seasoned with use, remember Surel Mitchell's inspiration for a live, work, create neighborhood in a shabby area of Garden City along the Boise River. Recognize the contribution and vision of real estate developer Jim Neill to build a Garden City riverfront subdivision on rundown industrial property previously used to slaughter livestock. Celebrate the teamwork of Boise City officials, individual private donors, and three locally grown nonprofit foundations to construct two new river-based parks. Be thankful for the willing participation of two irrigation districts to allow the use of farmers' water to thrill urban whitewater enthusiasts. Be mindful of the cooperation and leadership of two city governments to literally and figuratively build a footbridge from one side of the river to the other. Perhaps in time, these activities will be known as the perfect storm of economic development in the Treasure Valley: everything and everyone came together at exactly the right time.

SHEILA SPANGLER is a lifelong learner, experienced commercial lender, entrepreneur, and strategist accustomed to overcoming complex business challenges. She uses her intuition and creativity to find positive ways to influence people, process, and profit. She has a bachelor's degree in Multidisciplinary Studies with a minor in Communication.

7 | Crowding the Suburban Floodplain

At Eagle Island, developers build castles on sand.

by Emily Berg

In the 1940s, at Eagle Island 8 miles west of the Idaho Statehouse, the Boise River looped and wandered through a corridor of flood-swept marshland more than 1.5 miles wide. Today, there are subdivisions with levees that narrow the channel to the width of a four-lane road. Almost every new house near the river changes the pattern and risk of flooding. Paving the marsh for housing makes life near the Boise River more hazardous than ever before.

Historically prone to flooding, the future Eagle townsite remained mostly farmland and pasture before the era of the automobile. By 1910, canals and an electric streetcar spread housing west of Boise. In 1938, the State of Idaho founded an Eagle Island trout hatchery. The city's population topped 20,000 in 2012. "Developments are the story around here," Meg Carlson, long-time resident of Eagle Island, said. "Every year we have developers come in and offer to buy our property." As builders slate new developments in the floodplain (the flat area of land bordering the river), the risk of flooding is cumulatively increased both upstream and downstream. The increased risk of flooding has had little effect on land use decisions along the Boise River at Eagle Island, however, and developments continue to invade the floodplain.

One such development is Mace River Ranch. Polete Mace, one of the original founders of Eagle, settled at Eagle Island in 1887. In December 2012, the Mace family sold their 192-acre property to Gardner Company, which plans to build a new residential community, the Mace River Ranch on Mace Road. Set to house 218 home sites next to the Boise River, Mace River Ranch is just the next in the line of residential developments at Eagle Island.

Along with Polete Mace, many of Eagle's early pioneers gravitated to the natural island, known as Eagle Island, on first arriving in the Boise Valley in the late 1870s. This low-lying gravel island, with groundwater only a few feet below, sits between a north and south channel created by a fork in the Boise River. Eagle Island is more than 5 miles long from the split of the north and south channels to their convergence and

encompasses more than 3,000 acres. Annual flooding made the area lush and green. Cottonwood trees bordered both sides of the river, creating a natural wildlife refuge. Settlers thought it was the perfect place to start a prosperous farming operation to feed the growing population of Boise. Yet, because of the groundwater and surface water interactions at the island, river water inundated residents' homes and property every year. Cattle rancher T.C. Caitlin kept a boat moored to his porch to row to his barn when the floods came.

Head of Eagle Island

Within the past century, the lower Boise River downstream of Lucky Peak Dam, including the Eagle Island area, has been transformed from a meandering, braided, gravel-bed river to a channelized, regulated urban river that provides numerous benefits to the community but also poses some challenges. Perhaps nowhere on the Boise River has channelization been more dramatic than at Eagle Island, where the developments and commercial activities have altered the floodplain significantly. Whereas in the 1800s, the river was sometimes as wide as 900 feet, by 2002 the river had been reduced to only 140 feet wide at the head of Eagle Island. The construction of the three federal dams upstream substantially reduced downstream flows and increased channelization, allowing for activities such as gravel extraction and residential development along the river.

Despite the fact that the Eagle Island area is a floodplain, the City of Eagle has designated future land use there as residential development pursuant to Eagle City Code. In her job as county engineer and floodplain administrator, Angie Gilman oversees applications for developments within the floodplain. "That whole area is a floodplain. All the material underneath, all that property over there," Gilman said, pulling off the hood to her rain jacket and pointing out to the fields and subdivisions, "is nothing but sands and gravel just like you see here at the river bank." Building on rocky, permeable substrate such as that at Eagle Island can compact it and reduce its permeability. This, in turn, can hinder one of floodplain's most valuable functions: the ability to convey floodwaters. Channelization of the river, which increases river flow velocities, compounds the problem. Because of these factors, Eagle Island may be less able to withstand excess floodwaters, and flood damage may become more widespread.

In addition, the increased flow velocities can cause greater erosion and alter vegetation and fish habitat. Building in the floodplain inevitably alters that floodplain and changes the ecosystem of the river as well. This is not an effect that can be measured for each development, Gilman stated, but a cumulative effect that can't really be avoided unless development within the floodplain is prohibited entirely.

Allowing for the filtration of groundwater and surface water is one of the invaluable services that floodplains provide to ecosystems and communities. Infiltration improves surface water quality by removing nutrients and sediments. This process is inhibited by development on the floodplain, but water still flows through and can become a real problem when it comes to flood operations. Ellen Berggren, Boise project manager for the U.S. Army Corps of Engineers, said that the Eagle Island area can be inundated even during periods when the corps is releasing flows lower than flood stage from the three federal dams upstream. "At the Eagle Island area, they start having problems when the river reaches bankfull and even before. You have water running between houses and yards," Berggren asserted. "As a gravel bar with a high water table, even if the river isn't overflowing the banks and getting everywhere, the fact that the river is full means that the water table stays high and people have subwater and water in their backyards."

Flooding along the Boise Greenbelt

Eagle Island poses a real challenge for flood hazard mitigation for the Corps of Engineers and other floodplain administrators. Despite the risk of flooding, similar to the early settlers of Eagle Island, people today want to live next to the river and enjoy its beauty. There's a certain acceptance of risk among people who decide to build their homes at Eagle Island. Recurrent flooding is common, but there haven't been any catastrophic flood events or even substantial property damage to illustrate the real risk of living there. As further development is allowed on the floodplain, however, it will be increasingly difficult to manage floodwaters at Eagle Island and all along the Boise River. The flood hazard for the entire area adjacent to the river will continue to increase, and the degradation of the riparian ecosystem will escalate.

Banbury subdivision in April 2006

Regulations on Building in the Floodplain

Federal, county, and city regulations govern floodplain development at Eagle Island. At the federal level, the Federal Emergency Management Agency's (FEMA's) National Flood Insurance Program has set standards based on its own flood hazard mapping. Ada County has initiated even stricter requirements than the FEMA standards. For example, although FEMA allows developments in the floodplain as long as the developers show that their building projects will not result in raising the base flood elevation, Ada County allows no development at all in the *floodway* (i.e., the part of the floodplain that includes not only the channel where the current flows but also the area immediately adjacent to the channel that is susceptible to being inundated during flood events).

FEMA's purpose is disaster preparedness—their standards may keep houses from being swept away by a flood, but they don't allow for protection of floodplain functions or ecosystems. Regardless, FEMA maps are the basis for land use policy decisions in Ada County. Berggren said, "It is not necessarily good land policy. ... [FEMA] allows you to build in the floodplain as long as you elevate ... [but] as long as we're building and filling in the floodplain, we're altering the extent of the floodplain." Floodplain ordinances are essential for setting boundaries on development within the floodway and the floodplain, but the cumulative effect of decisions about land use on the floodplain is still largely ignored. The growing risk of greater flood hazard cannot be a factor considered by planning and zoning departments when they are relying on outdated FEMA maps for decisions on land use within the floodplain.

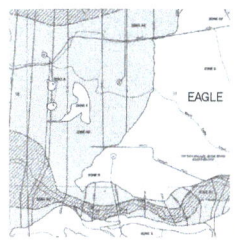

The gray areas of this 2003 FEMA map show the floodplain west and south of the City of Eagle—an area that continues to experience substantial residential growth since this map was released.

With the rate of development at Eagle Island, the cumulative effect of subsequent developments can be a challenge when relying on FEMA maps. As Berggren states, "The maps that FEMA completed are no longer valid. When you put more houses and fill in, the extent of the floodplain changes. You can't keep up with that when you're doing floodplain mapping." Because mapping floodplains is an expensive enterprise, Berggren said, it is only done every 10 years or so. New FEMA maps were scheduled to be released in December 2014. Prior to the release of these new maps, planning was based on maps that came out in 2003, based on data from 1997. Since that time, the floodplain has been affected by land developments, gravel mining, flood control projects, and flow regulation. Gilman commented, "I can pretty much guarantee [the new FEMA maps] aren't going to show that the floodway is any narrower! If anything, they're going to show that it's wider, because we now have more development and activities along the river." The floodplain will continue to widen with new developments, and more areas will be affected in the future. Some homes that weren't previously considered to be in the floodway will be included in the floodway in the new FEMA maps.

The story of Eagle Island begs for better land management practices. In addition to the risks and difficulty of having annual floods to residential areas, extensive gravel extraction and other factors have led to ecosystem degradation. Commercial and residential developments have led to bank instability and a greater risk of flooding. The Corps of Engineers is concerned with the risk of gravel pit capture, that is, when the river erodes into the gravel pit and changes its course. When the gravel pits are dug, only a tiny strip of land remains between the river and the pit. The river can quickly erode the strip if it jumps the bank. The result is that the entire

Eagle Island State Park

river flows into these pits, "totally changing the hydraulic head [i.e., the mechanical energy of the flow] and causing upstream and downstream erosion," as explained by Berggren.

Eagle Island State Park and Ecosystem Restoration

One effort to prevent more development on Eagle Island is Eagle Island State Park. On the site of a prison farm operated by the State of Idaho until 1977, Eagle Island State

Park, created in 1983, encompasses more than a fifth of Eagle Island at 545 acres. It boasts 5 miles of horseback riding and hiking trails, 9- and 18-hole disc golf courses, horseshoe pits, volleyball courts, and a waterslide. Shelters and grassy areas make comfortable picnic spots, and a swimming beach and paddleboard rentals enhance the park's recreational opportunities.

In 2006, Ada County Parks and Recreation Department came out with a master plan for Eagle Island State Park that would have significantly expanded the park. The plan called for the creation of additional lakes, new wetlands, and a series of channels throughout the park. Cottonwood forest and native plants would occupy the perimeter of the park. While providing some great opportunities for outdoor recreation for a growing population, the plan also provided for flood control measures and ecosystem preservation. The plan was subject to funding, however, and never materialized.

In another planning effort, the U.S. Army Corps of Engineers conducted a feasibility study in 2010 at Eagle Island that focused on ecosystem restoration for damage caused by gravel extraction and other encroachments on the river. The project sought to improve the wetland diversity at the gravel extraction pits and evaluated methods for doing so. The feasibility study examined the possibility of creating shallow benches along the pond areas for fish called dabblers, eradicating noxious weeds, and improving cottonwood regeneration. "We felt that by restoring and improving habitat, cottonwood forest, and native vegetation in that area," Berggren explained, "we could really reduce the risk of pit extraction and thereby the flood hazard for those living on the island," Although the study was shelved because of lack of funding, it calls attention to opportunities for better land practice at Eagle Island.

Great blue heron

Eagle Island needs habitat restoration and protection. The number of heron rookeries has declined on the Boise River because herons don't thrive in an atmosphere of disturbance or close proximity to people. Providing some open space away from development could improve their numbers. Fish populations are also negatively affected by developments along the river and the loss of riparian habitat. Cottonwood tree regeneration has been affected as well. In addition to encroachment on the river, other factors contributing to environmental degradation include the creation of dams upstream, pollution and sedimentation, and increases in water demand by communities and farmers. Providing for open space to be maintained in perpetuity would help protect the existing habitat and floodplain functions while also allowing for space for water to go during flood events.

Marsh corridors, flood lakes, landfill, stilts, and waterproof basements have all been proposed as alternatives to levees and dams. But the issue remains hotly contested. In 2006, after Eagle City Council approved another 54 upscale houses on Eagle Island, many Boise Valley residents feared the worst. "The madness continues," said an editorial letter to the Boise Guardian. "I don't think dikes or levees are the answer. You'll just be pushing water into somebody else's place." Flood zoning, like all zoning, has always been windfalls and wipeouts. The sandbagging of a subdivision seldom lowers the risk of flooding. It merely displaces the risk of flood.

EMILY BERG grew up in Boise, Idaho, where she's currently finishing up her undergraduate degree in environmental studies. She enjoys studying the intricate relationship between people and the environment.

Daylighting Caldwell

Urban renewal transforms an asphalt floodway.

8

by Dean Gunderson

On Sunday, December 30, 2001, Bryan Dines's life changed when a large portion of the building that housed his business Like Nu Car Wash collapsed into a mostly forgotten waterway, Indian Creek, in Caldwell, Idaho. Unfortunately for Dines, the portion of the floor structure under his car wash that had been built in 1911, along with the old corrugated iron and concrete deck, finally corroded from below. Its nearly century-long exposure to the rushing creek's water and humidity had taken its toll. And although many Caldwell residents were surprised that a business had suddenly collapsed into a forgotten waterway, Dines's insurance company was even more surprised. They, too, were not aware that the building had been built over a running creek. They simply refused to cover any of the damage.

Many Caldwell residents forgot about Indian Creek, but the small river still coursed its way under much of the community's downtown, under roadways, vacant lots, parking areas, and many downtown buildings. As the country grew more automobile dependent, Caldwell began covering portions of the creek to provide more street crossings and to make more land available for real estate development.

A History of Water and Steel

Caldwell was founded in 1883 on the sure knowledge that America's westward progress would continue unabated—and that this progress would roll on steel wheels over steel rails. The Oregon Short Line Railroad Company and its sister organization, the Idaho & Oregon Land Improvement Company, staked out a desolate corner of land located just east of the confluence of the Boise River and the smaller Indian Creek. The company's front man, Robert Strahorn, platted the new town's streets to run parallel to Indian Creek, which was smaller and less prone to flood than the nearby Boise River.

Strahorn named this new town after his business partner, Alexander Caldwell. Strahorn's wife, Carrie Adel, later wrote in her memoir about Caldwell, "['There was] not a tree, nor a sign of habitation on the townsite—on the white desolate glare and clouds of alkali dust—it looked like a place deserted by God himself."

Yet, for the Strahorns, this godforsaken tract of land struck a chord of entrepreneurial fervor, for this was not the only townsite they had founded for the railroad company. In addition to founding Caldwell, the Strahorns had also founded the county seat communities of Hailey, Shoshone, and Weiser in Idaho and Ontario in Oregon. All of the sites for these communities provided a critical asset for the railroad company: access to water for their steam locomotives from waterways that did not regularly flood to any great extent. In Hailey it was the Big Wood River, in Shoshone it was the Little Wood River, in Weiser it was the Weiser River, in Ontario it was the Malheur, and in Caldwell it was Indian Creek.

The railroad bought Robert Strahorn to Idaho where he founded several communities including Caldwell.

Some of these communities had larger nearby rivers to quench their railroad thirst, and they flooded every year, swelling over braided streams like vernal clockwork. But Indian Creek still held onto its own chaotic secret. It, too, occasionally flooded, especially when helped along by human activities in the form of raging irrigation water. In the early spring 1894, Orchard Dam burst. The dam had been constructed some 40 miles east of Caldwell along the course of Indian Creek, creating a reservoir in a natural depression. Water from the Indian Creek Reservoir was intended for surface irrigation of farmland, but when the dam burst, it sent mud-choked waters coursing down narrow Indian Creek, causing it to overflow its banks and flood much of the young town's Main Street.

In early spring 1910, a warm spell led to an early thaw of winter snow. This glut of water washed away a portion of the levee on the newly constructed New York Canal. The Reclamation Service, quick to avoid a disaster, opted to divert a portion of the high water down into Indian Creek. They sent messages to the residents and business owners of Caldwell by 3 a.m., giving the town a 7-hour head start to move to higher ground before the creek breached its banks. The water kept rising for another 8 hours. Before it was finished that spring, all of Caldwell's downtown streets were under more than 3 feet of water.

These floods were not natural occurrences; they had been caused by changes made to the hydrological network of the Boise River Valley, modifications made to divert natural waterways for agricultural surface irrigation.

Robert Edmund Strahorn and his wife, Carrie Adell Strahorn

The Slow Loss of Indian Creek

Early settlers in Caldwell viewed Indian Creek as a fortunate and beautiful waterway that graced the town. In 1906, the Forward Club, a women's group dedicated to improving the cultural and educational footing of the young town of Caldwell, had as one of its principle goals for the community the construction of "a greenbelt along Indian Creek."

The creek figured prominently in the social and civic life of Caldwell residents. With a burgeoning agricultural industry taking root, provided by ample surface irrigation water, the community regularly celebrated its newfound economic success with events held along Indian Creek. Yet an inadvertent impact of a growing agricultural industry was the community's reliance on the small creek to carry away the considerable waste flowing from farm fields, animal pens, and meatpacking plants. According to Lee Van De Bogart, project engineer for the City of Caldwell, when the town was founded, the average flow in Indian Creek was a mere 3 to 5 cubic feet per second

Downtown Caldwell in 1907

(cfs). Yet, by the 1920s, the flow rates had increased with the advent of agricultural field drainage and effluent to a peak of 270 cfs—a 5,400% increase! Even at its lowest point, before the irrigation laterals opened in April, the creek ran at 130 cfs. With so much waste choking Indian Creek, its reputation as a pleasant place to relax and its role as a centerpiece of the community faded.

As Dessie Cole, a longtime resident of Caldwell, recalled, "Caldwell just smelled to high heaven." The idea of Indian Creek, what was flowing through it, and what it smelled like was so repugnant that she and her husband kept the presence of the creek a secret from their young son. Even though they lived just across from the stream, their boy was almost 5 years old before he first saw Indian Creek.

Caldwell before Indian Creek restoration, about 1975

A Confluence of Cars

Soon, city leaders began a concerted effort to cover the creek. This would serve two purposes: it would make more land available for development within the city center, and it would encapsulate the atrocious smell of the once clean running water. Most important, it would open up additional crossings of Indian Creek to automobile traffic and eliminate the narrow wooden bridges that divided the city. Caldwell had become a car-oriented city that appeared to have no river at all. This allowed many surrounding farms and industries to increase their discharges into the creek since it was hidden from sight.

By the early 1950s, after the creek was encased as it went through the downtown area, it was only possible along the outskirts of Caldwell to catch a glimpse of Indian Creek—either east of town along 21st Street past the rodeo grounds along the train tracks, or west of town just before the creek flowed into the Boise River, next to the sewer treatment plant. You were forgiven if you thought the natural stream was simply an unnamed agricultural drainage lateral because it looked just like any number of other such ditches, overgrown with rushes along its steep, artificially straightened banks and devoid of wildlife.

Yet, with the passage of the federal Clean Water Act in 1972, industrial discharges into streams like Indian Creek were deemed illegal. Slowly, the waters of the stream cleared and fish and wildlife began to return. But by this time, almost two generations had passed since the community hid the creek, and many newer residents were unaware that a live stream ran under the very heart of their city.

Top on the List in the New Millennium: Dines's Former Car Wash

Just before the turn of the millennium, Garret Nancolas, the newly elected mayor of Caldwell, began to investigate ways to turn around Caldwell's declining downtown. Despite years of effort to improve automobile access throughout the downtown area, businesses had simply chosen to relocate.

To foster renewed interest in the community, Mayor Nancolas sponsored several college-led investigations that would look at possible innovations. One of these efforts was a design charrette, which included students from the Caldwell-based College of Idaho, the Idaho-Montana chapter of the American Society of Landscape Architects, and the National Park Service. This effort focused on planning for a network of parks and greenbelt pathways throughout the community and the downtown that had been recommended by the Forward Club in 1906.

Immediately after Dines's car wash had collapsed, Mayor Nancolas called a town meeting, asking the public what, if any, help the community could provide for this downtown business. The mayor had already declared a state of emergency to notify the U.S. Army Corps of Engineers in hopes that they could render aid. This was even more urgent, since Dines's insurance company had just notified him that it would not cover the loss.

As a result of this town meeting, the public agreed that the city would pay for the initial cost of the removal of the most precarious portion of the collapsed car wash building. The city paid $13,750 from the city's emergency fund and placed a lien on Dines's car wash property to ensure that the community would be repaid. Unfortunately, Dines ultimately had to surrender the property in lieu of repayment on the lien,

Other cities in the country, such as San Antonio, Texas, have revitalized their communities by creating public spaces along waterways.

confounded by an inability to pay accumulating property taxes on a business that could not operate. The City of Caldwell was able to acquire the property at a significant discount, allowing the community to focus restoration resources to what would become a small public park.

According to Caldwell City Council president Rob Hopper, the design charrette was a resounding success. "The technical expertise of the National Park Service and American Society of Landscape Architects, combined with the guidance of local residents and experts, resulted in a plan that will, for the first time, make our community vision a reality."

Tearing Down Walls, Righting Old Wrongs, and Bringing in the Sun

By September 2003, the first-ever Indian Creek Festival was held to celebrate the first portion of the Indian Creek to be restored—the segment approximately one block to the west of the collapsed car wash site. The celebration included the dedication of a public sculpture that decorated a new pedestrian bridge to a new landscaped plaza. The event was a 1-day event that was held in an adjacent parking lot.

"I'm amazed at how well it's come together and how much excitement it's created," Mayor Nancolas exclaimed. "Enthusiasm tears down walls." By the following year, the annual celebration had grown to a 2-day event. The kickoff for the celebration was the demolition of the last remaining portion of the old car wash building and the removal of the old corrugated iron and concrete floor, bringing sunlight to a portion of Indian Creek that had not been exposed to fresh air for nearly a century.

Long-time Caldwell resident Gina Lujack said, "It's going to be wonderful! It's been a real pleasure to witness that the city heads have all turned the same direction. No one is against this. I think that in the long run, this planned progress we have is going to be better than a boom!"

The community enjoys a revitalized downtown during the annual Indian Creek Festival.

Color fills the landscape during Caldwell's Winter Wonderland Christmas light display.

Over the next 3 years, the city worked to develop a set of guiding principles and ordinances that would reaffirm the importance of Indian Creek and the role it would play in the downtown's redevelopment. In June of 2007, 35 years after the adoption of the National Environmental Policy Act and

Construction begins in 2007 to uncover Indian Creek.

the Clean Water Act, the Environmental Protection Agency (EPA), which was charged with implementing the acts, awarded a $200,000 grant to the City of Caldwell to help in its effort to restore Indian Creek. Jim Werntz, Idaho Operations Office director for the EPA said, "Caldwell employed smart-growth principles ... (making the) Indian Creek restoration and creation of nearby green space the centerpiece of the downtown revitalization."

This is not to say the restoration of Indian Creek proceeded without a hitch. In 2008, coinciding with the announcement of a new redevelopment planning effort and the ribbon-cutting ceremony for the new park on the old car wash site, the Federal Emergency Management Agency (FEMA) declared that all of downtown Caldwell was at imminent risk of flooding.

Not to be thwarted, the city announced new incentive efforts to encourage downtown redevelopment. This city-funded incentive package would be available for any new downtown development and would include a 60% cost share for downtown streetscape improvements (such as lighting, benches, irrigation, and trees), a new $500,000 transportation grant, a downtown-wide Wi-Fi system, a police bike patrol rotation, and the potential reduction in permitting costs for LEED-certified buildings.

"One of the key reasons that we became interested in the Caldwell downtown was the Indian Creek project," said Skip Oppenheimer, president of Oppenheimer Development Corporation. "I think we pictured it being enormously attractive and important. It adds a very distinctive quality to downtown Caldwell. Very few cities have that to offer."

A funtional water wheel is a prominent feature along Indian Creek.

That year, the fifth annual Indian Creek Festival was held, and it had now grown to overshadow the Egg and Dairyman Days celebrations of the 1920s. In the 1920s, hundreds of people came to Caldwell for picnics and a massive tug-o-war across Indian Creek, a war between the "brains and brawns" of townspeople.

In 2009, after the city had spent nearly $200,000 to reanalyze FEMA's data and adding to it the new grade and flow information from the Indian Creek daylighting effort, FEMA agreed to downgrade the flood risk in downtown Caldwell. Perhaps not surprisingly, the key information that led to FEMA's change in position was the crafting of a partnership agreement between local governments, including both the City of Caldwell and the adjacent City of Nampa.

In this agreement, an old wrong was righted. The New York Canal would play a central role in the protection of downtown Caldwell. In 1910, the Reclamation Service had diverted water from the canal into Indian Creek to minimize flooding of properties due to a failure of a levee wall on the canal. This had flooded all of downtown Caldwell. Under the new partnership agreement, the very same gates on the canal—where it crosses the natural Indian Creek riverbed, about 14 miles east of downtown Caldwell, will be adjusted to accept any potential floodwaters that may inundate the downtown. This arrangement will ensure that during a flood, a minimum of 2,500 cfs of water flow will stay in the canal.

In 2010, Caldwell introduced further administrative streamlining to help encourage downtown redevelopment. This new "red carpet" treatment expedites the approval processes for new projects that meet certain energy-efficiency guidelines. Furthermore, if these projects help generate new jobs, help restore historic buildings, and adhere to more stringent design standards, the redevelopment projects could qualify for partial funding from the city's urban renewal agency.

In 2015, five full blocks of Indian Creek flow freely through downtown Caldwell. According to Eljay White, Caldwell's finance director and city treasurer, nearly $1.5 million each year, over the next 8 years, will flow from the city's urban renewal efforts, much of it capitalizing on the shining jewel of a restored creek. The City of Caldwell is now poised for a renaissance of its downtown as the beauty of Indian Creek brings pride to the townspeople.

DEAN GUNDERSON has a master's degree in community and regional planning from Boise State University. He has received regional and national recognition for his architectural, furniture, urban design, and sculptural work and is committed to improving the quality of life within his community through livable design.

9 | Draining Dixie

An urban-rural alliance is changing the way Boise manages waste.

by Michael Gosney

The purchase of 49 riverside acres is setting the political stage for wastewater innovation. In 2009, at the Dixie Slough near Parma, the City of Boise purchased the acreage for a project called the Dixie Drain. The drain would chemically treat water heavy with phosphates. It would also allow the wetlands to filter pollutants in ways once common before rivers were leveed and dammed. A bold experiment in wastewater engineering, the challenge is both political and technological: it requires a level of city-state-federal intergovernmental cooperation that, thus far, has eluded this libertarian region of an anti-federal state.

The Water Quality Dilemma

The Clean Water Act is the main piece of legislation that dictates regulation of pollutants in bodies of water in the United States. The legislation and its regulations set guidelines for developing permit requirements and effluent limits for discharge from point sources such as factories and wastewater treatment plants. However, according to Justin Hayes, program director for the Idaho Conservation League, "The Clean Water Act does a horrible job of regulating the discharges from what is called nonpoint sources of pollution." A classic example of a nonpoint source is a farm. "Think of agriculture," Hayes elaborated. "Acres and acres of agriculture in the Treasure Valley are sources that are virtually unregulated by the Clean Water Act." There is no specific point where all of the pollution enters the Boise River; it generally enters from the whole field as irrigation water is wasted.

Nonpoint sources of pollution are typically beyond the reach of regulation using traditional means. The Clean Water Act grants the Environmental Protection Agency (EPA) the authority to regulate pollution in bodies of water throughout the United States. Although the EPA has been granted authority to regulate point sources of pollution, it does not have that same authority when it comes to nonpoint sources of pollution. Steve Burgos, Boise City environmental manager explained, "Under the current regulatory framework of the Clean Water Act, the Environmental Protection

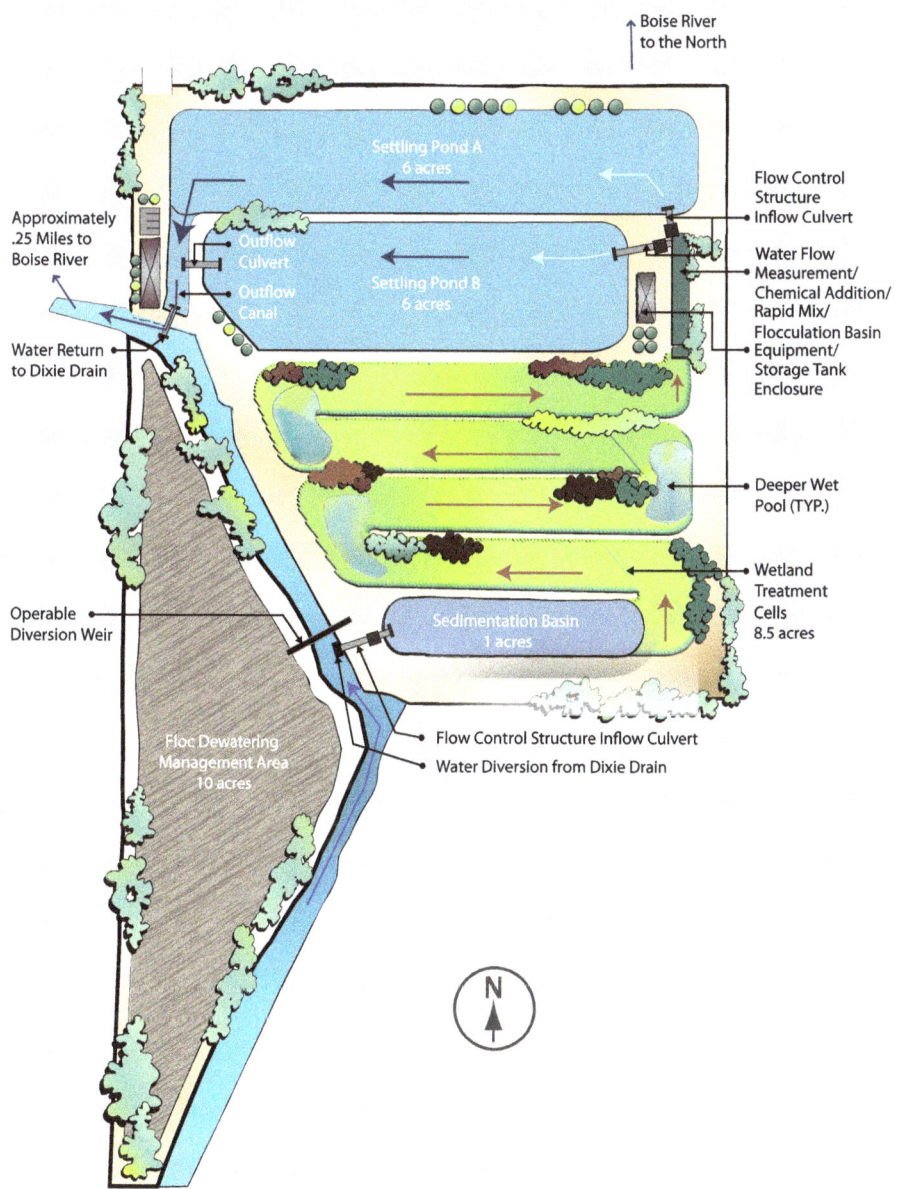

Agency has no jurisdiction to pursue environmental improvements on agricultural drains or to require some type of numeric limit on the discharge from a farmer's field."

A farm, being a nonpoint source of pollution, is therefore exempt from the Clean Water Act. Some farmers are careful to self-regulate their activities, but they are not legally obligated to do so. Hayes, with a concerned tone clarified this: "Farmers can cause almost any amount of sedimentation and other pollutants to be washed off their farm fields and not really be held accountable for that under the Clean Water Act."

As a result of the law and litigation of it, communities were left with water quality standards for rivers and streams that had been developed to address point source polluters. Although many states have tried diligently to address this pollution, ultimately the issue of nonpoint source polluters went unaddressed at the federal level. As a result, nonpoint source pollution was left to community Watershed Area Groups and Basin Area Groups, which have continuously sought to find solutions. Burgos explained that this problem plagued many communities throughout the country. "Probably the biggest challenge, and we see this in the Chesapeake Bay area too, is that you can take the point sources down to almost zero phosphorus, and when you run water quality models, you'll see that you may not be addressing the larger water quality issue because of the high levels of phosphorus in agricultural return flows."

Burgos pressed this point by explaining that there are 11 primary agricultural drains that flow into the lower Boise River. The EPA has no legal mandate to regulate any of these agricultural drains, and so they are essentially exempt from the Clean Water Act's standards. The EPA has no authority to regulate agricultural drains, and it cannot apply water quality standards to agricultural drains in an attempt to reduce pollution. As a result, the exemption of agricultural drains from the Clean Water Act is a severe obstacle to maintaining water quality standards.

Under the Clean Water Act, a city may be obligated to meet higher standards for point source pollution than the vague nonpoint standards. However, the standards placed on a city's discharge are often not enough to maintain positive overall water quality. "If you don't have some tools for tackling the agricultural runoff, you kind of throw the baby out with the bath water," Hayes said. To Hayes, ignoring nonpoint sources is counterproductive. "You can only make the city so clean before they're not really having an impact on the river anymore, but the river is not getting any better because the agricultural impact on water quality is going unaddressed."

Innovation Is the Solution

"The only entity standing around that has a legal obligation and can be held accountable for the discharge is a point source structure," Hayes said, "in this case, the City of Boise." Hayes explained that the Dixie Drain project created a unique opportunity for Boise. The city had an opportunity to pioneer innovative wastewater treatment, while continuing to meet its civic obligations. Hayes said that the Dixie Drain project allowed for the city to say, "We'll meet our obligation, but we'll do it in an innovative way where we'll put resources into treating the unregulated agricultural runoff problems." The City of Boise decided it would clean wastewater at the Dixie site to a greater degree than it was obligated to do at the city sewage treatment plant, where it had to deal with more expensive sewage-water point sources.

A brown current of nutrient-rich sediment flows from a 15-mile irrigation drain into the Boise River.

Marti Bridges, whose job as total maximum daily load (TMDL) program manager for the Idaho Department of Environmental Quality (DEQ) entails managing the process for developing water quality standards on nonpoint sources, provided further insight. She explained that a TMDL is "a water quality pollutant budget. It identifies how much capacity water bodies have for specific pollutants, which we then base allocations on." A TMDL is a critical component in conducting water quality nutrient trades, such as that proposed in the Dixie Drain project. "The City of Boise looked at moving water out of this agricultural drain and treating it," Bridges explained. "However, they looked at treating it in an innovative way with a mixture of a nonpoint source–point source treatment scheme."

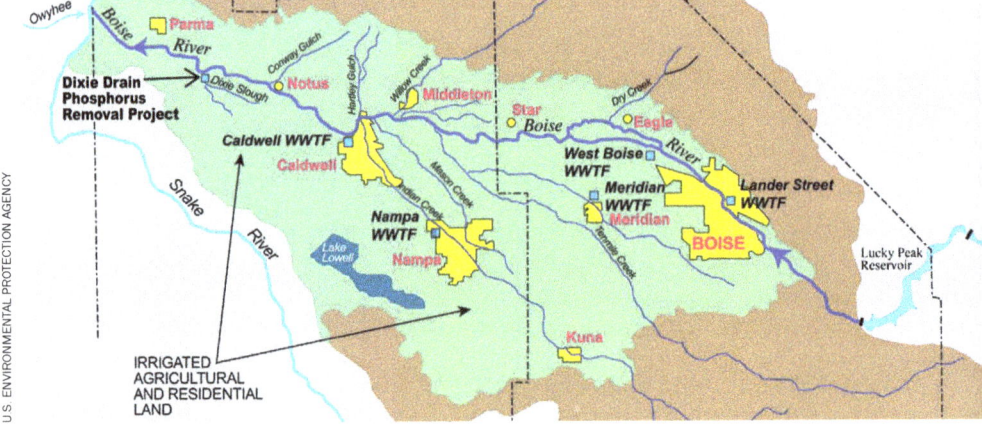

Dixie Drain settlement ponds will help the Boise River meet EPA water quality standards.

The City of Boise planned to use the Dixie Drain to address nonpoint sources of pollutants through an innovative trade system. This tradeoff would meet the nonpoint source pollution problem in the lower Boise and Snake River system. The trade would be arranged so that the City of Boise could remove a certain amount of phosphorus at the previously unregulated Dixie agricultural drain location in exchange for a reduction in their removal requirement at the city sewage wastewater treatment plant. "It's one of the first projects of its type that has been done, that I'm aware of," Bridges said, "and certainly the first of its kind in Idaho." However, before the city could move forward with this less expensive and innovative plan, it had to navigate a series of obstacles and criticisms.

Obstacles, Criticisms, and Concerns

Negotiation between the City of Boise and the EPA on the trade ratio was a critical step—an obstacle in the process of cleaning the Boise River. The exchange ratio had to provide "reasonable assurance" to EPA and the nation that the City of Boise would remove the necessary amounts of pollution at Dixie, located at the confluence of the Snake and Boise Rivers near Parma, to uphold their permit requirements. The agreed on ratio, explained Burgos, was "for every pound we were obligated to take out at West Boise, we would take out a pound and a half at Dixie."

However, before the City of Boise settled on the exchange ratio of 1.5 pounds for every 1 pound, they faced opposition from the Idaho Conservation League, a nonprofit organization. The Idaho Conservation League wanted the Dixie Drain project to proceed only if it had a net environmental benefit. "One of the ways that you can quickly figure out if it is having a net environmental benefit," Hayes said, "is by checking to see if it is causing more pollution to be removed from the river than would have happened under a different scenario." He added that the original version of the project was "only going to remove a fraction of the amount of pollution that the city was obligated to remove." The result would mean that the Dixie Drain would have a negative ratio net benefit to the environment. A negative ratio net benefit for the project meant that the trade would add to environmental degradation, instead of helping reduce it. That had to change.

The Idaho Conservation League did not have a favorable view of the project at this preliminary stage. "We were not enthusiastic about that at all," Hayes said. "The city felt like it could justify this position by looking at the way that water is diverted from the Boise River at different points of the river." The city thought that by diverting and treating water from different points of the river that suffered from greater degradation, they were justified in having the negative net ratio. "We felt like that was a loser proposal," Hayes said, "and we argued about that a lot."

The city eventually developed a positive ratio scenario. Hayes credited the development as a realization on the part of the city that if they wanted the project to move forward, it would have to have an obvious environmental benefit attached to it. Hayes stated that once the project developed the positive ratio, "It was very clear to us, and our supporters, that this was best for the river. With that, we decided we wanted to get behind it."

Wastewater is treated before being discharged into the Boise River.

Burgos claimed that the project initially received resistance from the EPA, as well as from the Idaho Conservation League. He credited a portion of the resistance to the fact that a project like this had not been done before. "We were asking for a pretty significant precedent-setting project," Burgos said. "It is a whole heck of a lot harder to pull something off like the Dixie Drain project and get it into a permit than it would be for them [the EPA] to just follow the normal path of an NPDES [National Pollution Discharge Elimination System] permit being developed for a treatment facility."

However, the EPA's initial skepticism of the project faded as the city improved the ratio of pollution reductions. The City of Boise provided a better explanation, to both citizen groups and regulatory agencies, of what the goal of the project was. The city reinforced its commitment to the goal of a cleaner river through means of developing a positive trade ratio and actively engaging and cooperating with the parties involved. As Burgos explained, "Once it was established that, in fact, this project has a better environmental outcome, it framed the project as one that we were all pulling in the same direction." After the city clearly established its intention, Burgos speculated that the EPA began to view the project more favorably and skepticism began to lighten. However, the project was then faced with the difficult legal obstacle of being fit into the regulatory framework of the Clean Water Act, which was originally passed in 1972.

"The Dixie Drain project is actually a very, very, complicated one," explained Mark Ryan, former assistant regional counsel for EPA Region 10. "The concept of trading the removal of agricultural drain phosphorus for reductions in the city's NPDES permit limits is fairly straight forward, but the devil, as they say, is in the details." Ryan explained that the Clean Water Act does not explicitly provide a framework for a project such as the Dixie Drain. As a result, it was necessary for the EPA to "reinvent a few of our standard procedures to make this work." The process took several hundred hours, but, Ryan added, "our management wanted this project to happen, so we worked really hard to figure it out."

In addition, the Dixie Drain project had received criticism from some members of the community as well. Criticism was directed toward the project being only a temporary solution to the phosphorus and nonpoint source pollutant issue. As Burgos put it, "There are certainly folks of the opinion that we're taking the quote, unquote, easy way out." Burgos added, "We feel an obligation as a public entity to take the route that is most cost effective and that optimizes environmental benefit."

Concerns over the project's potential for creating a phosphorus problem between the city's upstream wastewater treatment plant and Parma were focused on the precise location of the Dixie Drain treatment. The prime concern is that there would be a higher concentration of phosphorus in the river between Boise and the Dixie Drain treatment plant than would exist without the Dixie Drain facility. The City of Boise again supported the idea that this would be a better environmental outcome.

Hayes addressed the concern of higher phosphorus content as well. "Having the Dixie Drain downstream from Boise means that there is a segment of river between the two that is receiving a larger dose of pollution than it would receive had the City of Boise just met their obligation at the [upstream] sewage treatment plant." Hayes claimed that a project like the Dixie Drain should be located upstream from

Boise City Environmental Manager Steve Burgos, center, outlines the Dixie Drain project to the DEQ's Troy Smith, right, and EPA's Bill Stewart, left.

the city. However, because the city is at the upper end of the river, it would not be ideal in this particular situation. "It's not causing any water quality violations that would be considered unlawful or inappropriate," Hayes continued. "It is resulting in a degradation of water quality, not an unlawful degradation, but degradation nonetheless."

There were additional obstacles that concerned Bridges and Idaho DEQ. Similar to other parties involved, Idaho DEQ was initially hesitant about the Dixie Drain project. The reason for its immediate hesitation to provide support for the project was that the lower Boise watershed lacked an approved total maximum daily load, or TMDL. The TMDL plan had been ordered by a federal court in a 2002 settlement agreement that gave the state 10 years to complete dozens of TMDLs in Idaho.

Idaho DEQ had typically been opposed to allowing trades to occur without first establishing an approved TMDL. Without an approved TMDL in place, the parties involved would have to commit otherwise unnecessary resources to gather and analyze data on the proposed project, to ensure that it had a positive net environmental benefit. "Frankly, from an agency perspective," Bridges said, "we don't want to have to do a bunch of analysis for a number of Dixie Drain type projects. It's a huge time sink for staff and resources to do that, and it's much easier to do if you have a TMDL first." If a TMDL already existed, then the regulatory agencies would have a large amount of data to draw from, regarding which areas would benefit from trades, but the agency had dragged its feet in producing one.

Leading by Example

The parties involved in bringing the Dixie Drain project to life reaped a multitude of benefits. All of the parties involved stated that the project was beneficial to the river. Hayes explained that the Idaho Conservation League liked the project because it is treating "an irrigation return drain, which is an aggregated stream of water and contaminants." He added that while the project would be doing this, the water quality would be measured throughout the process. As a result, everyone will know precisely how much phosphorus was removed during treatment. The precise measurement of phosphorus treatment at Dixie allows for the city, DEQ, and EPA to verify that the city is meeting the requirements of the newly modified permit for the City of Boise at the city wastewater treatment plant. Hayes explained that this is a great benefit to the community because it ensures continued water quality. "If you fail to achieve the necessary amount of phosphorus reduction to meet your permit limits," Hayes said, "then you'll be in violation of your permit and you will be penalized for that."

The City of Boise also saw several benefits from the Dixie Drain project. The city benefited economically from implementing the Dixie Drain, and the river would be cleaned up. The City of Boise also benefited by gaining access to treating a previously untreatable source of phosphorus. This is significant for the city, because it is getting a better return on investment by treating a major source of phosphorus pollution. The city will remove more phosphorus at Dixie, per dollar spent, than it would have by purchasing immediate upgrades for the current wastewater treatment facility.

The EPA, DEQ, and the litigators of Idaho benefited from the project too. The EPA gained the benefit of receiving access to regulating a source of pollution that typically goes unaddressed and is considered a significant source of phosphorus. In essence, the EPA gained the ability to address nonpoint source pollutants as if they were a point source, which was not an option under current legislative framework and would have been a lengthy process to alter.

Bridges claimed that the DEQ benefited from the Dixie Drain project as well. The project was the sort of project that Idaho DEQ encourages. "We like to see proponents consider innovative projects," Bridges said. "They thought out of the box, and it wasn't the traditional type of strategy." The agency had hoped that the Dixie Drain project would serve as an example to both cities and agriculture throughout the state. DEQ claimed that the Dixie Drain served as a message to both municipalities and agricultural leaders that there are creative options for both trading and treating nonpoint source water quality concerns. "As an agency, we want to see all the cities in the valley improving their water quality from their discharge of pollutants," Bridges said. A goal of DEQ as a regulatory agency is to observe the reduction of pollutant levels in rivers and to benefit fish and wildlife. Bridges added that the Dixie Drain is evidence that this is achievable on agricultural drains.

For the people of Idaho and Boise, the Dixie Drain project is a home run. The project is a serious effort by the City of Boise to address phosphorus pollution in the lower Boise River, using an approach that many consider innovative.

It would be done at a cheaper cost than simply making a bigger, more expensive water treatment plant. The project has brought together several different parties and agencies in a collaborative effort to make a difference and produce tangible results. The end result is a project that provides municipalities, agencies, environmentalists, and the public with a tool to further improve the quality and efficiency of wastewater treatment. Best of all, the water in the Boise River will be cleaner tomorrow than it is today.

Officials commemorate the grand opening of a new water treatment plant in 2005 with the capacity to clean about 6 million gallons of Boise River water daily.

MICHAEL GOSNEY has a bachelor's degree (Boise State University) in political science with an emphasis on American government and public policy and a minor in history. His passions include writing, political education, raising political awareness, and advocating for political participation.

10 Wildlife Preservation

Parks and conservation protect the creatures of the Boise River.

by Mike Medberry

Celinda Hines rode into Boise along the Oregon Trail in 1853. She wrote that her group of wagon train voyagers "crossed over three bottoms reaching the river. The first is covered with sage, the second with woods, the third with grass." That green, green grass must have been a comfort to travelers after a long trip through the Great American Desert. She must have seen deer and antelope along the route from Missouri or Nebraska, sage grouse and rattlesnakes, grizzly and black bears, and perhaps thousands of bison along the way. Red-tailed hawks, ospreys, and eagles in the nearby trees beside the Boise River might have soothed her. No cows roamed the land and no cheatgrass grew, no dams loomed and nobody crowed about the need to protect the river because every acre that existed was simply wild. Hines had a fresh view of a harsh landscape and land that had not yet been tamed by the plow.

In the 1870s, fewer than 18,000 people lived in the Boise area. In 2015, roughly 616,500 people inhabit the Boise metropolitan area. In the past 100 years, the desires of white people have dominated development of land in the Boise River drainage and defined the course of floods. The Boise River has flooded at least 16 times over 100 years. Some of these floods were disastrous or near disastrous. Some of the high water was merely costly or inconvenient. Most of these floods occurred before 1944, and none has been more than 10,000 cubic feet per second since Lucky Peak Dam was built in 1955. Since the 1850s, wildlife have survived in good numbers, but some species, such as grizzly bear, salmon, and bison, have been wiped out while others have survived handily.

The Fort Boise Wildlife Management Area lies entirely within the Boise River floodplain at the confluence of the Snake, Owyhee, and Boise Rivers. When Lucky Peak Reservoir, which lies above the City of Boise, allows more than about 6,000 cubic feet per second of water into the river, the Fort Boise Wildlife Management Area is inundated. Apparently, the original Fort Boise was lost when flooding rivers changed course, but no one is really sure—call it lack of foresight or failed optimism, but today, this 1,300-acre piece of land supports enormous numbers of wildlife.

ADDISON MOHLER

The Fort Boise Wildlife Management Area features 13 ponds and 20 miles of walking trails along the Boise River. Andy Ogden, wildlife biologist for the Southwest Office for the Idaho Department of Fish and Game, said that Fort Boise is a popular place for duck, turkey, and pheasant hunting and is occasionally used for bass and catfish fishing. The area supports thousands of migrating waterfowl in the spring and autumn seasons, and occasionally rafters float through it to the Snake River.

A mallard duck takes flight.

Dam Building Brought More Wildlife

The U.S. Army Corps of Engineers and the U.S. Bureau of Reclamation have built 7 dams, 3 power plants, and 2,670 miles of canals and drains that turned the mostly dry Boise Valley into a place of abundant water. All of this work was done to control floods and provide irrigation between1915 and 1955, but today, as the valley fills up with people, the needs of people living here have changed in dramatic ways. Wildlife still thrive in the Boise area, partially because much of the water has been redistributed over a broader area over a longer period of time, but not everyone knows where to look for the birds and mammals.

"Humans in today's world are less connected to nature now than in any other generation and any other time in history," said Dave Cannamela in 2015. Cannamela is the superintendent of Idaho Fish and Game's MK Nature Center.

The 4.6-acre center, which sits right next to the Boise River beside Boise's 11-acre Municipal Park, offers educational programs and tours of the river area. "Sometimes people don't really know how much they enjoy nature," Cannamela continued. "They hear bird songs and are aware of the river, but they aren't really conscious of it all. They're out there walking, and, on some level, they know they need the river and water." The MK Nature Center has a native plant garden and sells plants in its annual auction in May, mostly to people who intend to plant their yards with desert-loving species like sage, bitterbrush, and wild rose.

Along the Morrison Knudsen Nature Center StreamWalk are sheltered areas to view wildlife in their natural habitat.

After World War I, Municipal Park provided a temporary place for people seeking to establish homesteaded claims on nearby land. The park provided a temporary place for people seeking to establish homesteaded claims on nearby land. Settlers brought their dreams to Boise, and some spent decades trying to "prove up" on the land, to make the land produce an income, mostly by farming and raising cattle. Some succeeded fabulously and some failed miserably, but most merely survived. Beaver were trapped out, dams were built, water was diverted, former floodlands were turned into farmlands, and wildlife flew or were driven away from the Boise River. Downstream dams blocked passage of salmon, steelhead, lamprey, and bull trout.

As the City of Boise developed in the early years of the 20th century, the need for parks to provide a connection between people and nature became increasingly important and wildlife returned to their home. In 1914, very few parks existed in Boise; in 2015, the city has at least 123 parks preserved mostly for people and wildlife to enjoy. The city government plans to add additional open lands to buffer the ever-expanding city.

When Lucky Peak Dam was built, the levees that were anticipated along the river were never built for lack of federal money. However, some private property owners who had land beside the lower Boise River built berms and levees with their own heavy equipment. It was done out of a fear that when the river changed its course, it would lay claim to their private land or make that land inaccessible. The levees were spotty—they were never built to uniform standards—and they forced floodwater onto other lands where water was neither wanted nor needed for farming. Where that water drained was never developed because the "surplus" land became swampy and the vegetation overgrown. Today, some of this land, including part of Eagle Island, is being developed on the ever-evolving floodplain thereby eliminating wildlife habitat.

Bald eagles look for prey.

Roosevelt's Refuge

Just west of the city of Boise, water at the west end of the 40-mile New York Canal formed Lake Lowell as a reservoir, and in 1909 the Deer Flat National Wildlife Refuge was proclaimed by President Theodore Roosevelt. Deer Flat surrounded the reservoir. It was formed to protect migratory birds, which were declining across the nation in the early 20th century. This protected refuge is now 10,588 acres and supports 249 species of birds, according to the U.S. Fish and Wildlife Service. The checklist includes many rare species, such as white pelicans, snowy geese, tundra swans, northern bobwhite, loons, merlins, peregrine falcons, and sandhill cranes. In winter, as many as 150,000 geese and ducks now roost at Lake Lowell, and predators, like bald eagles, are common. Before 1900, the reservoir site was dry and home to only a few desert birds and mammals.

Annette de Knijf, manager of Deer Flat National Wildlife Refuge, said that the area is popular with local people. "It's an urban area refuge in Canyon County with about 200,000 people and that's why this area is hopping!" She added that Deer Flat is an "overlay refuge," meaning that the land management is subservient to the primary use of water for the irrigation purposes of the State of Idaho, Bureau of Reclamation, and local irrigators. This presents a conflict with recreationists who want to use the reservoir for fishing, boating, hunting, and wildlife when water is drawn down for farming in the summer.

De Knijf also spoke about upland areas of the refuge, which are dominated by invasive cheatgrass that was brought in by cattle and sheep ranchers over a century. "The sage obligate species have been replaced by more weedy species." The sage grouse isn't listed as threatened yet, but lawsuits have been filed to support that listing and a decision is imminent from the U.S. District Court for the District of Idaho. The loss of sagebrush habitat across the West has profoundly affected the Boise River's wildlife, as cheatgrass displaces nutritious feed for the wild animals. "We would like to reestablish a sagebrush habitat type," de Knijf said, "but the cheatgrass is intractable." She was quick to add that the U.S. Fish and Wildlife Service is establishing test plots that may prove successful in getting rid of the cheatgrass by introducing natural bacteria to control it. This would encourage sage grouse, sage thrasher, pigmy rabbit, and antelope, among other species.

Annette de Knijf, manager of Deer Flat National Wildlife Refuge

The Deer Flat Visitor Center, near Nampa, Idaho, provides education about wildlife and history of the refuge in a series of dioramas. Starting from the visitor center, a 29-mile car trip around Lake Lowell Reservoir gives drivers a sense of the rapid pace of residential growth that has occurred over the past few years. Twenty-five miles of walking trails also depart from the visitor center. Some of the trails wander among the observation platforms, offering views of the lake and many varieties of birds. In 2015, a pair of bald eagles had roosted in trees along Lake Lowell, and the land was closed to curious people to protect the eagles for a few months.

The Star Walk

The Star River Walk is a mile-and-a-quarter stroll through woods and fields right beside the river near the town of Star. It is beautiful all of the way, although part of it must be rehabilitated to appear natural and that plan is currently in the works. Russ Renk pumped up his raft beside the river and readied for a fishing trip. Now an environmental consultant in Washington State, Renk and his brother Dan grew up beside the Boise River near Star. Renk said that he had a record of fish catches going back 50 years, complete with the names of fishing holes, species of fish, and changes to the Boise River. His "Fish Books" from 1960 to 1964 indicate that Russ consistently caught the following fish from the river: rainbow and brown trout, bass, whitefish, squawfish, chub, catfish, bluegills, perch, and carp on spinners and salmon eggs. In 1960, Renk took 97 fishing trips on the river.

Russ Renk catches an 18-inch rainbow trout on the lower Boise River.

Renk said that the lower river had changed significantly over many years, mostly from increased flows in the river, which he thinks changed the slow-water habitat from one that supported bass to swift, clear-running water that favors trout. The river supported squawfish, chubs, and carp 50 years ago and not much else when the river's flow was severely restricted, as the upstream dams were being repaired or maintained. What saved the fish when that water was shut off upstream was seepage from irrigation canals and the groundwater that rose in various places. As years went on, however, the Idaho Department of Fish and Game filed and won a lawsuit ensuring that water would be in the river on a year-round basis for all wildlife.

The Ribbon of Jewels

One of the premium places for Boiseans to see wildlife is in the 25 miles of bike riding trails on each side of the Boise River that form Boise's "Ribbon of Jewels," where people fish, float, and watch wildlife as they ride, run, and walk for exercise and joy. The parks, named after well-known Boise patrons, have been protected for 45 years; they include the Ann Morrison, Kathryn Albertson, Esther Simplot, Julia Davis, Barber, and Marianne Williams Parks. In addition, undeveloped pieces of land, such as the 1.6-mile Bethine Church River Trail, support riparian wetlands, wildlife nesting spots, and the river's fish.

Undeveloped portions of other protected areas support many wildlife species in the heart of the city. For example, young cougars dispersing from the foothills occasionally wind up along the river or the streets of Boise, but they are generally captured by Idaho Department of Fish and Game and released in habitats that are safer for these wild cats. Coyotes and wolves are more secretive and are seldom seen along the foothills; deer and red foxes are more commonly spotted. Kingfishers, magpies, great blue herons, snowy egrets, and dozens of different kinds of ducks can be seen on almost any day along the river within city limits. On the Boise State University campus, Canada geese, ubiquitous and protected, are yearlong residents.

Canada goose

It seems that the reservoirs, water diversions, and canals have been a boon for wildlife because where water is found in the desert, wildlife abound. But there remain three problems with the construction projects along the river: (1) many of the diversions have no screens on them and fish die in farm lands, (2) residential development now crowds the river and pushes back wildlife, and (3) created swampland now holds greater

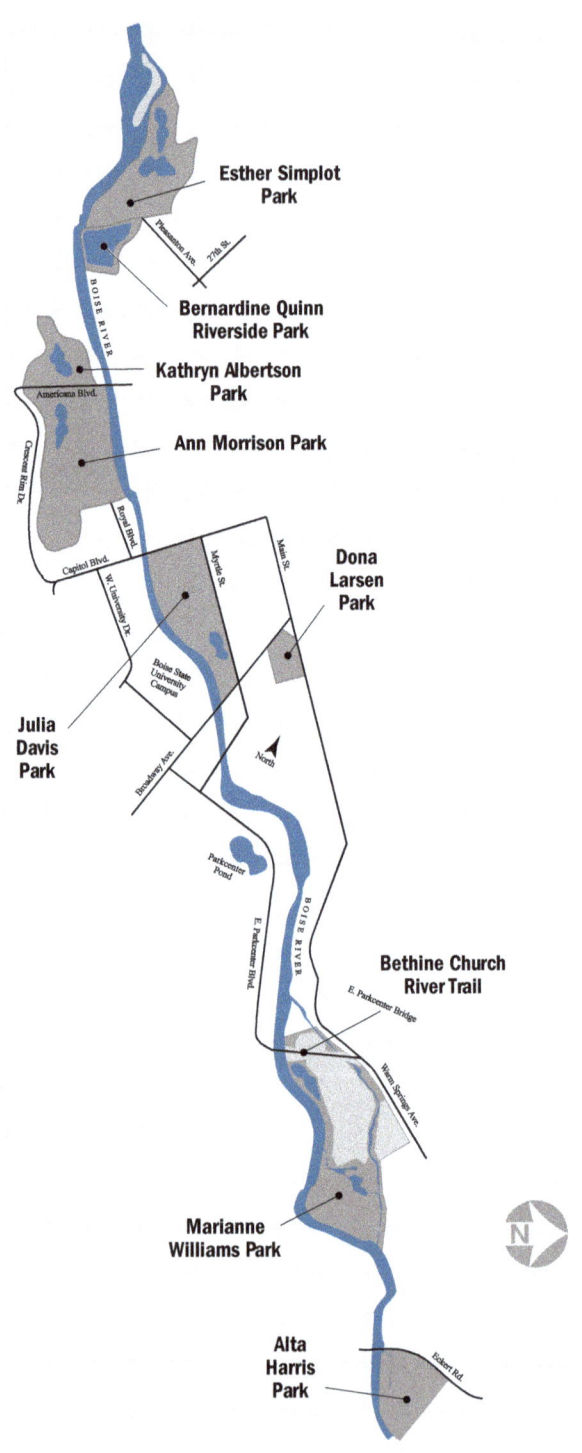

financial value and it is very expensive to protect wildlife. The pressure for controlling floods has also increased, with new subdivisions requiring more certain protection from floods, so that what was swampland might become dryland and then be sold as homeland. For the people who want to support wildlife, this trend is troublesome, and it is difficult to change.

American white pelican

The city of Boise will continue to grow, and the river that runs through it will continue flowing, but will we protect the habitat for pelicans, gopher snakes, and beavers? As long as the populace fails to assert its need for the river—for its beauty, productivity, and preservation of wild animals—the treasure that the Boise River embodies will shrink as home construction grows. Where the wildlife is still alive, the Boise River will remain a gorgeous place to visit right in the heart of the city. As Dave Cannamela said, "Sometimes people don't really know how much they enjoy nature." And the river speaks the final words: "until it is gone."

Beavers return to the Boise River.

MIKE MEDBERRY is a writer of short fiction, essays, and blogs, and teaches writing at the Cabin in Boise. He also wrote a memoir, *On the Dark Side of the Moon*, about recovering from a stroke he had while hiking in Idaho's Craters of the Moon National Monument. Look for him walking along the Boise River.

Selected Sources

Introduction

"Arrowrock Dam, Finishing Touch to Great Boise Irrigation Project." *Capital News* (Boise), October 4, 1915.

"Arrowrock Speaks." *Idaho Statesman*, December 2, 1931.

"Dam Is Monument to Senator Borah's Efforts." *Idaho Statesman*, September 26, 1915.

Morgan, Jane. "'Have Faith in God and U.S. Reclamation': Failure on the Boise Project, 1905-1924." *Idaho Yesterdays* 50, no. 1 (Spring 2009).

Reisner, Marc. *Cadillac Desert: The American West and Its Disappearing Water*. New York: Viking Penguin, 1986.

Chapter 1: Rain on Snow

Abramovich, Ron, Philip Morrisey, Jeff Anderson, Jeff Graham, and Alex Rebentisch. *Idaho Water Supply Outlook Report*, February 1, 2013. Boise, ID: USDA National Resources Conservation Service, 2013.

Bellingham, Keith. *What You Don't Know about Snow: The USDA's SNOTEL Network Is Playing a Critical Role in Protecting Water Resources in the Western United States*. Portland, OR: Stevens Water Monitoring Systems.

Ellis, Sean. "August Rains Boost Upper Snake Water Carryover." *Capital Press*, November 4, 2014.

Helms, Douglas, Steven E. Phillips, and Paul F. Reich, eds. *The History of Snow Survey and Water Supply Forecasting*. Washington, DC: USDA Natural Resources Conservation Service, 2008.

Marks, Danny, Tim Link, Adam Winstral, and David Garen. "Simulating Snowmelt Processes during Rain-on-Snow over a Semi-Arid Mountain Basin." *Annals of Glaciology* 32, no. 1 (2001): 195-202.

Marks, Danny, M. Seyfried, G. Flerchinger, and A. Winstral. "Research Data Collection at the Reynolds Creek Experimental Watershed." *Journal of Service Climatology* 1, no. 4 (2007): 1-12.

Moran, Joseph M. *Climate Studies: Introduction to Climate Science*. Boston: American Meteorological Society, 2010.

National Weather Service Climate Prediction Center. *El Niño – Southern Oscillation* (ENSO). http://www.cpc.ncep.noaa.gov/products/precip/CWlink/MJO/enso.shtml

USDA Natural Resources Conservation Service. "Snow Surveys and Water Supply Forecasting." *Agriculture Information Bulletin* 536 (1988).

Chapter 2: Raising Arrowrock

Barker, Rocky. "Idaho Wrestles with Water Issues." *Idaho Statesman*, February 4, 2014.

Community Planning Association of Southwest Idaho (COMPASS). *Products, Services, and Data - Special Projects - State Street Corridor*. http://www.compassidaho.org/prodserv/specialprojects-statestreet.htm

Federal Emergency Management Agency (FEMA). *National Flood Insurance Community Rating System: A Local Official's Guide to Saving Lives, Preventing Property Damage, Reducing the Cost of Flood Insurance*. Indianapolis, IN: FEMA, 2006.

Garden City Urban Renewal Agency. *River Front East Urban Renewal Plan*. Garden City, ID: Garden City Urban Renewal Agency, 2012.

Graham, Wayne J. "Should Dams Be Modified for the Probable Maximum Flood?" *JAWRA Journal of the American Water Resources Association* 36 (October 2000): 953-963.

Hoffman, Nathaniel. "Brownfields and Boise's 30th Street Area." *The Blue Review*, September 18, 2013.

Idaho Water Resource Board. *Comprehensive State Water Plan: Upper Boise River Basin*. December 1992.

Idaho Water Resource Board. *Idaho Flood and Seismic Risk Portfolio* (Effective 2012-2017). Boise, ID: Idaho Water Resource Board.

Lane, Nic. *The Bureau of Reclamation's Aging Infrastructure*. Washington, DC: Congressional Research Service, 2008.

Lovin, Hugh T. "The Carey Act in Idaho, 1895-1925: An Experiment in Free Enterprise Reclamation." *Pacific Northwest Quarterly* 78, no. 4 (October 1987): 122-133.

Morris, Donald L. "Value Engineering—Arrowrock Dam Outlet Works." *SAVE International Conference Proceedings* (1998): 275-284.

Stacy, Susan M. *When the River Rises: Flood Control on the Boise River, 1943-1985*. Boulder: University of Colorado, 1993.

Urban Land Institute. *Sustaining Agriculture: Measuring Success*. Boise, ID: Urban Land Institute, June-December, 2011.

U.S. Army Corps of Engineers, Walla Walla District. *Lower Boise River Interim Feasibility Study: Water Storage Screening Analysis*, August 2010. http://www.nww.usace.army.mil/Portals/28/docs/programsandprojects/lbrfs/BoiseGlScreenDoc_FINAL_Rev_2010.pdf

U.S. Army Corps of Engineers, Walla Walla District. *Lower Boise River Interim Feasibility Study: Preliminary Evaluation of Arrowrock Site*, October 2011. http://www.nww.usace.army.mil/Portals/28/docs/programsandprojects/lbrfs/BoiseGlArrowrockPrelimAnalysisReportOct2011.pdf

U.S. Army Corps of Engineers, Walla Walla District. *Boise River Feasibility Study*, 2014. http://www.nww.usace.army.mil/Missions/Projects/LowerBoiseRiverFeasibilityStudy.aspx

U.S. Department of Agriculture. 2012 *Census Volume 1, Chapter 2: County Level Data*. Washington DC: USDA Census of Agriculture, 2012.

Chapter 3: Water, Earth, and Gender

Armstrong, Jamie, and Laura Woodworth-Ney. *Culture of the Irrigated West: Complete Text: Introductions and Poems*. Boise, ID: Boise State University, 2014. http://education.boisestate.edu/irrigatedwest/text-poems

Benson, Jackson J. *Wallace Stegner: His Life and Work*. New York: Viking, 1996.

Brøgger, Fredrik Chr. "Wallace Stegner and the Western Environment: Hydraulics, Placelessness, and (Lack of) Identity." *European Journal of American Studies* 6, no. 3 (2011): doc. 5.

Cragg, Barbara Taylor. *Landscape Perception and Imagery of Mary Hallock Foote*. Missoula: University of Montana Scholarworks, 1980.

Floyd, Janet. "A Sympathetic Misunderstanding? Mary Hallock Foote's Mining West." *Frontiers: A Journal of Women Studies* 22, no. 3 (2001): 148-167.

Foote, Mary Hallock. *The Last Assembly Ball, and the Fate of a Voice*. Boston: Houghton, Mifflin, 1889.

Foote, Mary Hallock, and Rodman W. Paul. *A Victorian Gentlewoman in the Far West; The Reminiscences of Mary Hallock Foote*. San Marino, CA: Huntington Library, 1972.

Maguire, James H. "Western Writers Series: Mary Hallock Foote." Boise State College, 1972.

Reynolds, Susan Salter. "Tangle of Repose." *Los Angeles Times*, March 23, 2003.

Rodman, Paul W. "When Culture Came to Boise: Mary Hallock Foote in Idaho." *Idaho Yesterdays*, 20, no. 2 (1976).

Stegner, Wallace. *Wolf Willow: A History, a Story, and a Memory of the Last Plains Frontier*. New York: Viking Press, 1962.

Stegner, Wallace. *Angle of Repose*. New York: Penguin Books, 1992.

Stegner, Wallace. *Where the Bluebird Sings to the Lemonade Springs*. New York: Random House, 2002.

Chapter 4: Float, Paddle, and Surf

"Drenched Jaycees Survive Riotous River Raft Race." *Idaho Statesman*, July 12, 1959, p. 6.

Neil, J. Meredith. *City Limits: The Emergence of Metropolitan Boise, 1945-2001*. Unpublished manuscript.

Otter, J. "Boise Take Rapid Strides for Cleaner City." *Statewide*, September 29, 1949, p. 9.

Russell, Betsy. "Boise's Whitewater Park Thrives." *Spokesman Review* (Spokane), September 4, 2012.

Webb, Anna. "Two New Boise Parks All about Water." *Idaho Statesman*, November 29, 2011.

Chapter 5: History along the Greenbelt

Longsworth, Basil N. *The Diary of Basil N. Longworth* [sic]. Portland, OR: Historical Records Survey, 1938.

Planning Research West. *Boise River Greenbelt: Comprehensive Plan and Design*. Boise, ID: Planning Research West, 1969.

Strahorn, Carrie A. *Fifteen Thousand Miles by Stage*, ed 2. New York: G.P. Putnam & Sons, 1915.

Tuck, Kathleen. "The Boise River Greenbelt: Polishing an Urban Gem." *Urban Research: Occasional Papers of the Boise State University School of Public Service*, May 2014.

U.S. Bureau of Reclamation. *Reclamation Project Data: A Book of Historical, Statistical, and Technical Information of Reclamation Projects*. Washington, DC: U.S. Government Printing Office, 1949.

Chapter 6: The Waterfront District

Bieter, David. *Remarks to Idaho Environmental Forum*, August 13, 2014.

Boise River Park Donors. http://parks.cityofboise.org/parks-locations/parks/boise-river-park/donors

Crabb, Peter. "Tax Breaks to Lure Business Do Little to Spur Idaho's Growth." *Idaho Statesman*, April 16, 2014.

Crisp, Andrew. "Surel's Place." *Boise Weekly*, June 13-19, 2012.

Friends of the Park. *Boise River Park*. www.boiseriverpark.com

Hoffman, Nathaniel. "Rethinking the Void." *SSPA Research: Occasional Papers of the College of Social Sciences and Public Affairs*, Boise State University, January 2014.

Neil, J.M. "Gambling in Garden City: A Foot-Wide Town." *The Blue Review*, September 17, 2013.

Page, Tim. "Boise River Dams Built for Irrigation Not Flood Control." *Idaho Statesman*, February 23, 2014.

Simonds, William J. *The Boise Project*. Denver, CO: Bureau of Reclamation History Program, 1997.

Chapter 7: Crowding the Suburban Floodplain

"Another Flood Plain Subdivision." *Boise Guardian* RSS. May 17, 2006. http://boiseguardian.com/2006/05/17/another-flood-plain-subdivision

City of Eagle. *Special Flood Hazard Area Residential Requirements*. http://www.cityofeagle.org/vertical/sites/%7B78557FDD-14BE-414E-8624-C15ED40E9C6A%7D/uploads/Special_Flood_Area_Residential_Requirements(1).pdf

Harper, Robert W., and E.F. Hubbard. *Winter Water: The Flooding at Boise, Idaho, January 11-12, 1979*. Washington, DC: U.S. Geological Survey, 1980.

Hart, Arthur. "Floods at Eagle Island Were Annual Events." *Idaho Statesman*, May 30, 2006.

Idaho Silver Jackets. "Lower Boise River Flood Risk Community Meeting," June 19, 2012. http://www.nfrmp.us/state/docs/Idaho/BoiseFloodRiskCommunityMeeting19June2012.pdf

Smardon, Richard, and John Felleman. *Protecting Floodplain Resources: A Guidebook for Communities*, ed 2. Washington, DC: Federal Emergency Management Agency, June 1996. U.S. Army Corps of Engineers, Walla Walla District. Boise River Feasibility Study. April 2014.

Chapter 8: Daylighting Caldwell

"Caldwell Helps Owner of Car Wash That Collapsed into Indian Creek." *Idaho Statesman*, January 9, 2002.

Carlson, Brad. "Caldwell Moves to Revise Zoning." *Idaho Business Review*, November 28, 2005.

Doran, Sherrill, and Dennis Cannon. "Cost-Benefit Analysis of Urban Stormwater Retrofits and Stream Daylighting Using Low Impact Development Technologies." In *Proceedings of the Water Environment Federation*, 3833-3837. Alexandria, VA: Water Environment Federation, 2006.

"EPA Awards City of Caldwell $200K for Indian Creek Work." *Idaho Business Review*, June 4, 2007.

Forester, Sandra. "Canyon Officials Want a Creek to Run Through It." *Idaho Statesman*, April 2, 2002.

Forester, Sandra. "Workers Remove Car Wash Debris from Indian Creek." *Idaho Statesman*, April 8, 2002.

Forester, Sandra. "Revitalizing Indian Creek, Revitalizing Caldwell." *Idaho Statesman*, September 27, 2003.

Forester, Sandra. "Wrecking Ball Will Pump New Life into Caldwell Inside."*Idaho Statesman*, September 25, 2004.

Grigg, Dani. "Dedication of Indian Creek in Caldwell Only a Beginning." *Idaho Business Review*, May 5, 2008.

Idaho Department of Environmental Quality. "Case Study: The Caldwell-Karcher Design Charrette." In *Taking Plans-to-Action: State of Idaho Nonpoint Source Management Program Annual Report*, 2002.

Johnson, Rochelle, and Cristina F. Watson. *Rediscovering Indian Creek: The Story of Our Region*. Caldwell, ID: Caxton, 2004.

Leppert, Elaine C., and Lorene B. Thurston. *Early Caldwell through Photographs*. Caldwell, ID: Caldwell Committee for the Idaho State Centennial, 1990.

Volkert, Lora. "Caldwell Mayor Garret Nancolas: Indian Creek to Be Diverted This Month." *Idaho Business Review*, January 14, 2008.

Chapter 9: Draining Dixie

Barker, Rocky. "Feds, State, Locals Unite against Pollution through the Dixie Drain Project." *Idaho Statesman*, July 2, 2014.

Carlson, Brad. "Boise Aims to 'Reopen' Just-Updated EPA Sewer Plant Permits." *Idaho Business Review*, April 4, 2012.

"EPA Region 10 Administrator Visits Dixie Drain; Idaho's Congressional Delegation Urges EPA to Support Approval of Lower Boise Phosphorus Removal Project." *States News Service*, July 7, 2010.

Frenzel, S. A. "Effects of Municipal Wastewater Discharges on Aquatic Communities, Boise River, Idaho." *Water Resources Bulletin* 26 (April 2007): 279-287.

MacCoy, Dorene E. *Water-Quality and Biological Conditions in the Lower Boise River, Ada and Canyon Counties, Idaho, 1994-2002*. Reston, VA: U.S. Department of the Interior, U.S. Geological Survey, 2004.

Chapter 10: Wildlife Preservation

Arkle, Robert S., David S. Pilliod, Steven E. Hanser, et al. "Quantifying Restoration Effectiveness Using Multi-Scale Habitat Models: Implications for Sage-Grouse in the Great Basin." *Ecosphere* 5, no. 3 (2014): 1-32.

Benda, Lee, Daniel Miller, Paul Bigelow, and Kevin Andras. "Effects of Post-Wildfire Erosion on Channel Environments, Boise River, Idaho." *Forest Ecology and Management* 178 (June 2003): 105-119.

Busbee, Montague W., Benjamin D. Kocar, and Shawn G. Benner. "Irrigation Produces Elevated Arsenic in the Underlying Groundwater of a Semi-Arid Basin in Southwestern Idaho." *Applied Geochemistry* 24 (May 2009): 843-849.

Hines, Celinda E. "Diary of Celinda E. Hines." *Oregon Pioneer Association Transactions* 46 (June 20, 1918): 115-116.

Kofoed, Clair. *Fort Boise Wildlife Management Area: Management Plan*. Nampa: Idaho Department of Fish and Game, July 2003.

Rieman, Bruce E., and John D. McIntyre. "Occurrence of Bull Trout in Naturally Fragmented Habitat Patches of Varied Size." *Transactions of the American Fisheries Society* 124, no. 3 (May 1995): 285-296.

U.S. Fish and Wildlife Service. *Deer Flat National Wildlife Refuge, Idaho*. Nampa, ID: Deer Flat National Wildlife Refuge, March 2007.

www.ingramcontent.com/pod-product-compliance
Lightning Source LLC
Chambersburg PA
CBHW040334300426
44113CB00021B/2752